HOW TO HOOK A LITERARY AGENT

Stephanie J Hale

www.stephaniejhale.com

Copyright
Copyright 2010 Stephanie J. Hale
Reprinted: 2017

www.stephaniejhale.com

ISBN: 978-0-9928460-9-1

The moral rights of the author have been asserted.
All rights reserved. Apart from any fair dealing for the purposes of research or private study, or criticism or review, as permitted under the Copyright, Designs and Patents Act 1988, this publication may only be reproduced, stored or transmitted, in any form or by any means, with the prior permission in writing of the copyright owner, or in the case of the reprographic reproduction in accordance with the terms of licences issued by the Copyright Licensing Agency. Enquiries concerning reproduction outside those terms should be sent to the publisher.

Powerhouse Publications
94/124 London Road,
Oxford
OX3 9FN

Print Edition

British Library Cataloguing in Publication Data.
A catalogue record for this book is available from the British Library.
Cover design, editing, formatting by Oxford Literary Consultancy

Contents

Chapter 1: Programme Yourself For Success
The importance of goal-setting and a winning attitude. 7

Chapter 2: Convincing Agents Your Book Will Sell
Take away the guesswork – collect your facts and figures. 17

Chapter 3: Free Tools On The Internet
Market research in three minutes. 25

Chapter 4: The 12-Second Decision
How branding sells books… and how to use this to your advantage. 31

Chapter 5: Getting Inside Your Reader's Mind
Who is your target reader? How to create a connection. 39

Chapter 6: How Agents And Publishers Think
What are YOUR book's selling points? 44

Chapter 7: Creating A Buzz About Your Book
Use the right buzz words to sell your manuscript. 51

Chapter 8: Preparation Is Everything
Enticing agents to read your book. 58

Chapter 9: The 'Must Have' Submission Letter
Dos and don'ts for your covering letter. 66

Chapter 10: Selling Yourself
Building your professional credentials. 77

Chapter 11: Write A Sensational Synopsis
Writing a synopsis that leaves an agent hungry for more. 86

Chapter 12: Start With A Bang, Not A Whimper
Is the opening of your book strong enough? 97

Chapter 13: Spit and Polish
Editing and revision – a quick checklist. 110

Chapter 14: First Impressions
Lay-out and presentation of your manuscript. 117

Chapter 15: Who To Send To
Targeting the agents and publishers most likely to accept your book. 123

Chapter 16: Publishing Etiquette
How many submissions? What agents really mean. 129

Chapter 17: Rotten Rejections
Inspiring success stories. 134

Chapter 18: Agent Or Publisher?
Agent or publisher: the pros and cons. 144

Chapter 19: The Magic Of A One-Line Pitch
The magic of a one-line pitch. 149

Chapter 20: Your First Meeting
How to prepare. What to ask. 154

Chapter 21: When To Hassle, When To Hold Fire
Troubleshooting. 161

Conclusion: Live Your Dreams
You can do it! 163

For my children Cormac, Tierni and Chiara who shine light on the world each and every day

Chapter 1

Programme Yourself For Success

The Importance of Attitude

There was once an unknown writer whose book had been rejected by over 30 publishers.

His self-belief was so strong that he ignored these 'experts'. He wrote out a cheque for one million dollars and boldly wrote his name on it. He stuck this to the ceiling right over his bed so that it was the first thing he would see every morning when he woke up.

He mocked up a copy of *The New York Times* bestseller list. He placed his book in the Number One slot and left copies around his home in prominent places. He attached one to his shaving mirror, and tucked another under the sunshield in his car.

The experts had all told him that his book would not sell. But he went ahead against their advice and self-published it anyway.

Ordinary people bought the book and loved it. Just over a year after being launched, his book was on every major bestseller list in the United States and Canada.

That unknown writer was Jack Canfield, co-author of *Chicken Soup For The Soul.*

To date, over 100 *million* copies of his book have sold in 40 different languages. Total retail sales have reached $1.3 billion.

Just imagine what would have happened if Jack Canfield had given up on his thirtieth rejection... if he'd succumbed to despair, tucked his manuscript under the bed and gone back to his 'day job'.

You're Not The Only One

If you've been rejected by a literary agent or publisher, don't despair. You are far from alone. The list of famous and successful authors who have faced rejection from publishing experts is seemingly endless.

It includes the likes of: George Orwell, F. Scott Fitzgerald, C.S. Lewis, Beatrix Potter, Jack Kerouac, Vladimir Nabokov, Stephen King, Salman Rushdie, John Grisham, John Gray and Robert Kyosaki. Often, the rejection was harsh and the readers' comments were brutal.

Yet these supposedly unmarketable authors went on to publish classics or bestsellers. They achieved fame, acclaim and literary awards in spite of their critics!

Check YOUR Mindset

Before you start this home study programme, it's worth checking out your own mindset and attitude.

Ask yourself:

- Do I believe in my book?
- Am I passionate about my writing?
- Do I want to get my 'message' out to the world?
- Am I willing to keep going in the face of obstacles?
- Can I ignore naysayers?

- Am I ready to recover from my mistakes?
- Am I able to learn new skills?
- Am I prepared to do whatever it takes to achieve my goals?

The right mindset is absolutely crucial to your success. If you answered 'yes' to at least four of these questions, you're over half-way there!

Right from the start, I'd invite you to see rejection as part of your journey as a writer. Once you develop this attitude, you'll see it as a learning process rather than letting it crush you.

More importantly, you'll have the ability to persevere and keep going, rather than giving up like so many other writers.

What Are Your Goals?

One of the first questions I ask my clients is: "What do you hope to achieve by writing a book?"

Here are some of the answers I get:

- I am writing to make money.
- I want to help other people.
- I want my book to be turned into a film.
- I'd like to win literary prizes.
- I'd just like to see my book in a bookshop.
- I'd like to be famous.
- I want to generate more leads for my business.

- It will help establish me as the 'go to' person in my profession.

These are important answers because they will help you to set clear goals. I recommend that you set both short-term and long-term goals.

Once you have clear goals, you can work your way backwards and decide what steps you need to take to reach your destination. You can identify the gaps in your knowledge that need to be filled. You can decide what compromises need to be made. You can also decide which tasks you will do yourself and which ones you'd prefer to outsource to freelancers.

You can also decide whether or not your goals are realistic.

Your Reticular Activator

Your reticular activator is the part of your brain that filters out information. It makes you notice some things and ignore others. Without it, you'd be totally overwhelmed by the competing stimuli around you.

This part of the brain stays on alert 24 hours a day, even though you're probably not aware of it. Its decisions are based on survival instincts plus anything else you think of as really important.

You can use your reticular activator as a powerful force in your life. Give it a strong, clear goal and your brain will go to work for you round the clock, helping to find a way to make it happen.

And yes, writing fake cheques for yourself and mocking up bestseller lists with your name at the top help to stimulate this too!

Where Are You Right Now?

Many writers who seek advice are at their wits' end. They have sent out their books to literally hundreds of agents without success. They are often close to giving up.

They may have written perfectly publishable manuscripts – but often, these haven't even been glanced at by agents or publishers. My clients know this and some have devised clever tricks - such as putting hairs between pages of the manuscript - to see if their sample chapters have been read!

I have helped these writers and I'm confident I can help you.

Your Second Chance

If you follow my guidelines, it's possible to repackage your work and send it back to the same agent or publisher. If you've done the job properly, they are unlikely to even recognise your submission.

You may even find that an agent or publisher who has previously rejected you suddenly wants to take you on. This has happened to many of my clients over the years, so I know that this is perfectly achievable.

I should clarify here that this guide is <u>not</u> intended to help you write a publishable manuscript. There are enough books, evening classes, and courses that focus on how to structure a plot, write in a compelling style, and so forth.

I am assuming you will already have done this research before committing pen to paper (or sitting down in front of your computer)!

Getting Your Foot In The Door

Ninety-five per cent of writers aren't using my success strategies – and won't even know about them. When they approach agents, they are shooting themselves in the feet and both hands too. What's worse, they don't even know it!

Some of the top literary agents and publishers are getting nearly 1000 manuscripts per WEEK – and only 3 per cent of these books are getting accepted. If your book is to have a chance, then you need to stack the odds in your favour.

How To Hook A Literary Agent contains more than 20 years' of publishing knowledge and experience condensed into one home study programme. These are the secrets I've used to help so many writers find literary agents and get their books on editors' desks.

The quickest I've ever achieved this was in under one hour with a leading agent in New York. More often, it's taken me around seven days.

Obviously, I can't guarantee you'll get the same results in the same time frame. But I know for certain that I can offer you behind-the-scenes insights into the way that agents think... which means you can make your submission package so much more appealing.

Going The Extra Mile

You are looking for an edge in a fiercely competitive market. To succeed, you have to be prepared to do things that other writers aren't doing, aren't prepared to do, or don't know how to do.

I'll help you to identify your blind spots, and enable you to correct mistakes you may have unintentionally made in the past. My aim is to give you frank, honest, and professional advice so that your manuscript has the best chance possible.

As with most things, brilliant results aren't achieved without a little grit and elbow grease. However, your hard work will be rewarded. You'll be learning skills that will serve you well throughout your writing career.

So, without further ado, let's get started!

What Next?

Exercise One

i) What is your primary motivation for writing your book?

ii) What are your short-term goals with your writing?

iii.) What are your long-term goals with your writing?

Exercise Two

i) What gaps in your knowledge do you need to fill in order to fulfil your goals? (E.g. Public speaking, PR, marketing, internet marketing, etc.)

ii) Which of these skills are you willing to learn rather than outsource to someone else?

iii) How will you do this? (E.g. Find a coach or mentor / attend a seminar / read a book.)

iv) Which of these skills will you need to outsource? (Eg. Hire a freelance publicist/copywriter.)

v) How will you do this? (Useful on-line resources for recruiting help are: www.elance.com / www.rentacoder.com / www.hiremymom.com)

Exercise Three

How can you stimulate your own reticular activator? (E.g. Write your own imaginary cheque. Mock up your own bestseller list. Write up your Number One goal and tape it above your desk.)

Chapter 2
Convincing Agents Your Book Will Sell

Many writers get so caught up in the whirlwind of writing their book, they don't stop to consider their target audience – or if they do, it's a secondary consideration.

They see it largely as the publisher's job to find readers for their book.

A small percentage of writers will even go so far as to tell you they're just writing "for themselves".

That's all very well if you want to self-publish your book, and if you're not bothered about book sales, but you have to think a little differently if you want to impress a literary agent or publisher.

Do Readers Want *Your Book?*

Consider this: 70 per cent of published books don't make a profit or earn back the advance that was paid for them. That means only 30 per cent of books are making money!

In most industries other than publishing, this would spell disaster! You can therefore see why agents and publishers might be preoccupied with finding books that will sell!

So, what is the best way to grab an agent's attention? You guessed it! Convince them that there are people who want to read your book.

In order to do this, you need to think about *who* is likely to buy your book and *why* they are going to be interested in it.

Here are some of the questions you need to ask yourself:

- What proof or evidence is there that people will buy my book?
- Have they bought other similar books or publications in the past?
- Are there books similar to mine on Amazon that are selling well?
- Are large numbers of people looking up my subject on Internet search engines?

Check Out The Competition

The best way to see what is unique and special about your own book is to look at other similar books. A quick search on www.amazon.com will soon reveal: how other books are being marketed; what reviewers are saying about them; how up-to-date (or not) they are; and who their target audience is. Is *your* book filling in any 'missing pieces' from these other books or do you have a new angle to offer? Are you saying anything controversial or busting open any myths?

I recommend that you keep a 'swipe file' of reviews or synopses that you particularly like. You can then dip into this for ideas and inspiration when it comes to writing your own jacket blurb or sales page.

Take Away The Guesswork

Research facts and figures that will build a case for your book. For example, if your book is about golf, find out the number of golfers in the world or how many golfing books are purchased annually.

If your book is about Reiki, get statistics for the number of complementary therapy practitioners or people who seek natural healing or circulation figures for a leading holistic health magazine.

If you have written a romance, find out how many romance novels sell each year, and how many reading circles or internet forums are linked to this particular genre.

The Internet can help no end with this sort of research. Just type the relevant words into a search engine such as www.google.com. Statistics that might have taken hours to find are there at the touch of a button. Sites such as www.wikipedia.com are also great tools; though there are hundreds of other viable alternatives.

Market Research On The Internet

Other valuable tools for your research – particularly if you are writing non-fiction – are the Google Keywords tool and the Google Trends tool.

You can use these free tools to find out exactly how many people are searching for your subject – or your 'keywords' – each month.

These tools are so important that I've devoted a separate chapter especially to them. (You'll get to this in a moment.)

If you haven't used either of these tools before, then you're in for a treat!

Use Sparingly!

These numbers are a vital part of your pitch as they draw attention to the potential audience for your book.

How many copies of your book would be printed? How many books could be sold? What profits are likely to be made? Without such research, figures can only be plucked from thin air.

However, well-researched statistics enable literary agents and publishers to visualise the market and readership. They take the guesswork away. Your research also shows them that you're a professional and you take your work seriously.

A quick word of warning: you're aiming to give **ONE** relevant statistic (or possibly two) that will highlight your potential readership. Do NOT swamp your submission with figures!

What Next?

Exercise One

Look at an online bookseller's website or visit your local bookshop. Look at your competitors.

i) How are these books being marketed? (Colours, book cover images, blurb, etc.)

ii) Who would you say these books are being targeted at? (Age, gender, class, education, etc.)

iii) What are reviewers saying about this book? (Both good and bad.)

iv) What is your book offering that theirs does not?

v) Put together a 'swipe' file of any blurbs or book reviews that you would particularly like to refer to at a later date.

Exercise Two

i) What proof or evidence do you have that readers want *your* book?

ii) Are there any magazines, clubs, internet forums, or blogs dealing with your particular subject area or topic? List them.

iii) Are there any circulation figures or membership figures that are relevant? List them.

Exercise Three

i.) Is there a bestselling book aimed at a similar target audience to yours? What is the book's title and who is the author?

ii) How is this being marketed and towards what sort of readership is it being targeted?

iii) How many copies have been sold?

Exercise Four

Review the statistics you have collected. Which ONE is your most impressive – and relevant - statistic?

Chapter 3

Free Tools On The Internet

Market Research In Under Three Minutes

Wouldn't it be wonderful if you could pinpoint exactly what your readers are *most* interested in, what they are *least* interested in and what their priorities are?

Wouldn't it help, just a little bit, with selling your book? I mean, it'd be like gold dust, right?

In the old days, market researchers had to stand on street corners with clipboards, jotting down this information. Then they had to wade through thousands of questionnaires.

Nowadays, there is a wonderful little tool on the Internet that can give you the results in seconds.

Your FREE Marketing Tool

Google's Keyword tool is pure treasure for savvy writers. Even better, it's absolutely free. No, don't switch off because it sounds too techie - this is a simple online tool that ANYONE can master.

This tool is most powerful for non-fiction books. (Though this isn't to say you couldn't use it with fiction and poetry.)

Here's how it works. Every day, millions of people around the world search the Internet for whatever subject is of interest to them. They usually do it by typing what are known as 'keywords' into Google. Luckily for us, Google converts all these searches into monthly statistics. So, at the touch of a button, we can find out who is looking for what.

Stay with me! I'll give you the link to the keyword tool in a moment. But for the time being, let me explain how this might work.

What Do Readers REALLY Want?

Google Keywords

Suppose, for example, you're writing a book about caring for pet dogs.

You can simply type the phrase 'pet dogs' into the keyword tool. You will then discover that 368,000 people are looking for the phrase 'pet dogs' each month.

That translates to over four million searches per year! Here's when it gets exciting, because Google doesn't just show you how MANY people have been searching for your keywords, it also tells you the EXACT words and phrases they are using.

At the time of writing this guide, 'dog health' has 18,500 searches in contrast to 'dog disease' which has 8,100. 'Dog training' has 22,200 searches and 'dog grooming' has 165,000 searches. These statistics give me important information about what readers are most likely to be interested in. In other words, what readers REALLY want – as opposed to what I *think* they want.

This tool can be used to plan the contents of your book and your chapter headings. It can be used when you're preparing your pitch for an agent. You can use it if you're setting up a website to promote your writing. Later on, you can use it when you're writing press releases.

Try out the Google Keywords tool now. Type in the keywords that tie in with your book. See if you can gain any useful insights. Think about how you might use this information to make your book more marketable.

The address is:

>https://adwords.google.com/select/KeywordToolExternal

Google Trends

Another useful tool when you're selling a book or planning a marketing campaign is the Google Trends tool.

Writers often wonder: when is the best time to launch a book? Who exactly wants to read it? Where in the world are they based? What is their primary language?

All this information is just a few clicks away with the Google Trends tool.

You can find it by typing this web address:

>www.google.com/trends

The neat thing about this tool is that it keeps a record of what people are searching for when they type keywords in Google. It then compiles graphs from these statistics.

We will use the keywords 'keep fit' as an example of a book genre. If you type these words into the box provided at Google Trends, you will see that a five-year graph instantly pops up.

Looking at this graph, you'll notice that there's a sharp 'spike' at the beginning of every year. This is around the time people start making New Year's Resolutions. So if you were writing a health and fitness book, it would make sense for a publisher to launch it around this time.

Underneath the graph, there is a breakdown of the countries - and cities - in the world where the majority of these word searches are being made.

At the time of writing this article, the country making the most searches for 'keep fit' is the United Kingdom, closely followed by Hong Kong and Malaysia.

The top cities are Milton Keynes, Watford and Sheffield. So if you're an author planning a book tour – real or virtual – this information is invaluable.

Go ahead now, and type in the keywords for your own book. See if Google Trends can give you any useful insights.

Has interest in your subject risen or declined over the past five years? Or does interest stay fairly constant over time, with little blips around holiday periods such as Christmas?

Both these tools can help to give you the edge over other authors when it comes to selling and promoting your book.

What Next?

Exercise One

Use the Google Keywords tool to check the number of monthly global searches for your main keywords.

i) How many people are searching for your main keywords each month?

ii) What are the top associated keywords?

Exercise Two

Use the Google Trends tool to research your keywords.

i) Has interest in your subject risen or declined over the past five years?

ii) Are there certain times of year when people are more likely to look for your particular subject?

iii) Where in the world are your readers most likely to be located?

Chapter 4
The 12-Second Decision

Understanding Genre

When you enter a bookshop or an online site like Amazon, thousands of books are vying for your attention. To help customers make a choice, similar books are grouped together and packaged in a similar way. These groupings are widely called 'genres' and 'sub-genres' – though on Amazon they are called 'categories' and 'sub-categories'. One of the main purposes of a *genre* or *category* is to brand a book so that a reader can find it easily.

Understanding Branding

You will notice that book covers are often branded in similar ways, based on their genre or category. Chick Lit, for example, has a tendency to appear in bright colours such as lime green, cerise or tangerine. There's usually a zany typeface and a caricature illustration. Historical romances often have a beautiful woman in period costume on the front. Literary fiction regularly employs black and white photographs with a slightly somber feel.

Individual publishers also create their own branding to help market their books. Look at the orange border on books in the Penguin classics range. Virago, too, has done a fine job of marketing women's fiction in dark green covers with the famous apple symbol.

It Takes How Long?

This is extremely clever branding. If you have never thought about this before, then do so now. These colour-coded and symbolic messages are designed to give buyers at-a-glance information about a book before they even open the cover.

Bear in mind that the average reader takes just 8 to 12 seconds to decide whether or not to buy a book. Yes, that's right – it takes longer to floss your teeth than it does for the average reader to decide whether, or not, to part with their hard-earned cash!

What Agents Are Thinking

Agents and publishers are all too aware of this. When you send them a manuscript, they are most likely thinking the following:

- How are we going to sell it?
- Who are we going to sell it to?
- How will it be packaged or marketed?
- Which genre or category does the book belong to?
- Are there any similar books and how well have they sold?
- Where will the book fit in our current 'list' of books?

Bulk Buying Decisions

In fact, it may surprise you to know that many bookshops and libraries think like this too. I have been present at many book selection committees over the years. (These are the committees where decisions are made about which books to buy.) Do they read the books cover to cover before they purchase them? Do they even open the book covers?

Do they heck!

Often, the very first thing they do is to research the number of times a book – or a particular author - has been issued to readers or purchased by readers in the past. In other words, they check out an author's track record.

If you have no track record, they will look at similar subjects or authors to see how popular they are with readers.

Do You Need To Re-Brand Yourself?

This is why first-time authors sometimes have an advantage over old-timers. 'Mid-list' authors, whose books have shown only mediocre sales in the past, are finding it very tough nowadays. One bad year of book sales can create a 'foregone conclusion' about all future book sales. This then becomes a self-fulfilling prophecy.

Sometimes it is best for 'mid-list' authors to use a pseudonym and re-launch their careers. This personal re-branding enables them to start again with a clean slate.

Talent Will Out

OK, your hackles may be rising already. This may all sound a bit harsh and brutal. You may prefer to think in more altruistic terms. Deep down, you may believe that publication should depend solely on a book's literary merits or that a writer's talent should shine through.

I can only tell you that I have known many talented writers

over the years who have resisted advice about marketing their manuscripts. They have hated the idea of their books being pigeon-holed into specific 'genres' and 'categories'. They have believed that branding and marketing dumb down their writing and undermine their 'higher' principles. However, their books have yet to see the light of day and that is a great tragedy.

I can also think of many average writers who have succeeded beyond their wildest dreams because they firmly embraced the idea of branding and marketing their books. They researched their market. They found out what their readers wanted most. They made it their mission to learn what agents and publishers were looking for. Then, they delivered exactly that.

How To Use This Knowledge To Your Advantage

Once you understand how 'publishing' operates, you can use this knowledge to your advantage. I had a client several years ago, for example, who had written a book of poetry.

Poetry rarely makes money and is incredibly difficult to sell. We 're-framed' these poems as daily meditations or 'thought bites'. This, combined with the writer's own powerful personal story, meant that the book could be slotted into the 'self-help' genre (which is much more marketable). As a result, a mainstream publisher finally offered a deal for this 'impossible-to-place' book of poetry.

The question is: does the content of your book need 're-framing' in some way? Or can you rewrite your pitch in such a way that it will be irresistible to publishers?

What Is Your Genre?

Books sell better if they belong to a specific genre. This is because everyone knows what the score is. Agents and publishers know who is most likely to buy a book and how to locate them and attract their attention.

Readers know exactly what they are getting and where to find it. They will usually have bought several similar books already.

To help you decide into which genre your book fits, I have compiled a list of genres. This is not a complete list. There may well be many more that you can think of. With some books, the answer will be instantly apparent. With others, you may find that a book is a hybrid of several genres.

If your book fits into two or more genres, it may make the most sense to focus on the one with the most commercial appeal.

Genres

- Adventure
- Autobiography
- Business
- Chick Lit
- Children
- Cookery
- Crime
- DIY
- Erotica
- Fantasy
- Finance and Investment
- Gardening
- Gothic
- Historical
- Horror

- Humour
- Law
- Literary
- Picture books
- Poetry
- Political
- Psychology
- Reference
- Romance
- Saga
- Sci-Fi
- Self-help
- Short stories
- Spy
- Supernatural
- Teenage
- Thriller
- Travel
- War

What Next?

Exercise One

i) Which genre(s) does your book belong to?

ii) Does it fit into a specific genre? Or is it a hybrid of two genres, such as an historical romance or literary travel?

Exercise Two

i) Can you 're-frame' your book or pitch it in such a way that it sounds more appealing (or marketable) for literary agents and publishers?

ii) If you have published a book before and your sales were low, does it make sense to 're-brand' yourself with a different pen name?

Chapter 5

Getting Inside Your Reader's Mind

Who Are You Writing For?

"I'm writing for everyone!"

These are the words that strike terror into the hearts of even the bravest literary agents and publishers!

Everyone? What, *every* man, woman and child, regardless of age, interests, hobbies, income, educational level or life experience? How are you going to find these readers? How are you going to target your book campaign? Oh yes, *every*one is going to be *every*where!

That's going to be one hell of an expensive marketing campaign! No wonder publishers turn pale and look like they're about to faint!

OK, let's be serious for a minute.

Some of the best marketing campaigns are aimed at a very narrow niche readership. In fact, the more specific you can be, the easier your readers will be to identify and target.

As a result, your advertising and book marketing is likely to be much more effective.

Even better, agents and publishers will love you for it.

Who Is Your Target Reader?

For a powerful marketing campaign, it helps no end if you, as author, can be crystal clear about your target reader. Get inside their head. Understand their thoughts and preoccupations, their deepest desires and yearnings, their fears and anxieties.

What sort of language and vocabulary do they use? What are their biggest problems? Why are they likely to buy a book from you? Where do they 'hang out' offline and online?

This will help you on a fundamental level when it comes to pitching your book to an agent or publisher. It will also help you when your book is hot off the printing press and it's time for you to start promoting it.

So, here is a quick list of the things you need to be clear about:

- What gender and age is your 'ideal' reader?
- What is their educational level and likely income?
- What do they do in their spare time?
- What sort of books or publications have they bought already?
- Which e-zines, blogs or forums are they likely to read online?
- Which radio / TV programmes do they tune in to?
- Which clubs / organisations / membership sites do they belong to?
- What conferences / events are they likely to attend?
- What are their three biggest frustrations or problems?
- What are their three biggest hopes and dreams?
- What outcome are they hoping for when buying your book?

- The biggest reason they would buy from me would be…

Connecting With Your Readers

One of my clients – a prime-time TV celebrity – went through the above list with me a couple of days before he went on BBC radio to promote his new book (which was aimed at women in their 40s).

He felt his previous media interviews hadn't been strong enough as he hadn't been getting many sign-ups to his newsletter. Listening to him, I felt he was pitching himself in too highbrow a manner. He was connecting intellectually, but not emotionally. I felt he needed to talk with the same warmth and intimacy, and using the same informal language, that he would with a female friend or his sister.

By strange coincidence, a close friend called me shortly afterwards and it turned out that she'd heard this author on the radio. The interview had touched her so much that she'd stopped her car by the side of the road to listen – something she'd *never* done before in her life.

This is the power of knowing – and understanding – your target audience. You can move people so much that they'll drop whatever they're doing and listen to you.

And yes, they'll also buy your book.

What Next?

Exercise One

i) Answer the bullet points above. Are these reluctant or avid readers? Do they want a page-turner to read on the beach, a quick fix to a problem, or are they looking for something a bit more challenging?

Exercise Two

i) If you were given the task of promoting and selling your book at a grass-roots level, where would you start? (E.g. Could you promote it with your parent-teacher association / a heart foundation charity / a sports club / a local business network?)

Exercise Three

i) If your ideal reader heard you talking about your book on the radio, why would they be most likely to stop to listen to you?

ii) What emotions would they be experiencing?

Chapter 6

How Agents And Publishers Think

How Publishers Think

Reality Check No.1. Publishers want to make money. The days when major publishing houses – and indeed, literary agencies - served as fairy godmothers to new and worthwhile talent are long gone.

If a publisher is going to the expense of editing and typesetting your book, designing a cover, printing several thousand copies, and distributing it around the country, not to mention the 70 per cent discounts demanded by some book stores, they want to be fairly confident that they can sell it.

Anything else would be lunacy!

They not only want to cover their expenses (which are extensive) but also, ideally, make a profit. It will help them (and ultimately you) if you can show them *why* your book is going to sell and *how* they are going to sell it. And yes, you guessed it, there's much more to this than simply identifying your genre and target readership!

How Agents Think

It's a risky business being a literary agent. You're not paid upfront and you only get paid for your successes.

Even then, you only take 10-15 per cent commission of your client's advance (or 20 per cent for foreign sales).

So supposing they get you a book deal of around £25,000.

That's approximately £2,500 to cover all their expenses.

Let's break this down, so that you have a clearer understanding of where agents are coming from.

Your average business has all sorts of expenses at the end of each month: office costs, telephones, stationery, postage, accountancy fees, staff salaries, advertising, etc. A literary agency needs to generate enough profits to cover these costs.

Most manuscripts that agents read are looked at *gratis*, without any payment at all. All expenses and risks are initially incurred by the agent. You, as author, pay them nothing until your book is sold.

If you want to hook a literary agent or publisher, it's essential that you see the world through *their* eyes.

It's hardly surprising that they opt for books that seem marketable with a clear target audience. Basically they are looking for books that will SELL!

Why Do People Buy Books?

There is something very clever about advertising. Something so insidious, that it's worth examining in greater detail. We know we're being manipulated. We know we're being enticed and entranced.

We resist. We turn off the TV. We turn over the page of the magazine. We shrug off temptation, muttering: "I'm not falling for that!"

Yet every now and then an advert will catch us off-guard. It will somehow resonate with us. You'll find yourself, seemingly against your will, hankering for a chocolate bar, ordering a toy from a mail order catalogue, or calling a plumber who carried an advert on the side of his car. Why? There's a question and a half. That's how fortunes are made – and that is why it's worth examining this phenomenon in more depth.

Look At Adverts Around You

Spend an hour or so observing adverts around you – be they printed or broadcast commercials. All adverts are relevant, whether they are selling cars, washing powder or baby nappies!

Look at individual adverts and pinpoint exactly *how* they are working. In other words: what are the selling points? Occasionally, these selling points are explicit, but just as important are the *implicit* messages.

Examples Of Explicit And Implicit Selling Points:

- This will help fulfil your dreams - glamour, wealth, health, prestige, etc.

- You have a problem. This is the solution to your problem.

- If you're passionate about your hobby or pastime, you'll buy this.

- This will provide you with fantasy and escapism.

- This is THE most up-to-date product.

Now, let's briefly explore the motivations that prompt Joe or Josephine Public to buy a product. In other words, *why* are they likely to respond to marketing messages?

Examples Of Buyers' Motivations:

- Escapism – longing to get away from the mundane and ordinary.
- Pain – need to solve a problem (health, emotional, relationship, etc.)
- Gain – desire to improve appearance, intellect, finances, career, etc.
- Habit – familiarity. Bought something similar in the past.
- Passion – already has an established hobby or pastime.

Emotions Sell Products!

The interesting aspect to all this is that the majority of decisions aren't based on need, intellect or rational thinking. They are based on *emotion*.

An advert may simply 'strike a chord' or 'press the right buttons'. In other words: *emotions sell products*.

Products - such as your manuscripts or book - do not have to be highly original or unusual in order to sell (although obviously this helps). Often it is enough just to tap into an emotion, to capture the imagination, or to arouse curiosity.

This can be done through various triggers and carefully selected words. I call these words 'buzz words' because they are like tiny electrical shocks, stimulating people's emotions.

The principles you've learned so far are going to be invaluable as we progress through this home study programme.

Having got this far, I can confidently say that you're already streets ahead of most other writers. The majority never think of their books as 'products'. They don't think in terms of sales or marketing. When they finish writing their book, they see this as the 'end', rather than the 'beginning'.

Hopefully, you'll see how this attitude holds them back.

Admittedly, it does take time and effort to master these strategies. But the rewards will prove their worth many times over.

What Next?

Exercise One

i) What are my book's main selling points?

ii) What are my book's explicit / implicit marketing messages?

iii) Why will readers be motivated to buy my book?

iv) What sort of emotions will they be experiencing when they read my book's blurb?

Chapter 7

Creating A Buzz About Your Book

Every Word Counts

The advertising industry spends millions of pounds each year researching the impact of individual words and phrases. Adverts are continually tweaked and changed. Sometimes the alteration of a *single* word or letter in an advert can double the sales figures.

The phrase 'how to' has proved to be one of the most effective sales points in a book title. The insertion of a simple point of punctuation – the question mark – has also been shown to have a dramatic impact on sales. Researchers have found that adverts that evoke strong visual images and colours have more impact than those that do not.

This has massive significance for us. Every word has power. Every word has persuasion. Every single word in your submission package – from your book title to your biography – should be working as hard as it can on your behalf.

Choosing Your Buzz Words

I mentioned the importance of buzz words in the last chapter – words that are likely to trigger emotional responses and actions.

To do this, we're going back to the medium we're most familiar with – the printed word. So pop to your local shop and take a look at the news stand.

Look at the headlines and sub-titles on the newspapers and magazines. Look at a variety of publications to give you a good overview – sports, cars, gardening, business, health and beauty, for example.

You should also look at 'tabloids' (mass market sensationalist newspapers) as well as 'broadsheets' (the more serious newspapers).

Whatever you may think of the popular press, you cannot doubt its power. One only has to look at their circulation figures to see that these wordsmiths know exactly how to bait their hooks and reel their readers in.

Occasionally, I find resistance to this exercise. You may be thinking: "What on earth does this have to do with my travel guide for students?" or "I haven't written a trashy novel full of sex and violence!" Bear with me. You're developing a new skill that's going to help you to sell your book. Stick with it, do the exercises, and all will eventually become clear.

Your initial task is to jot down words that grab your attention, arouse your curiosity or provoke emotions. Don't worry about the 'rights' and 'wrongs' of this. Silence the inner critic telling you which words you should or shouldn't respond to.

You may find, for example, that you are more interested in the latest sex scandal with an England football player than in the Government's latest summit on climate change.

Remember, though, that buzz words appeal to our emotions rather than our intellect. These buzz words may be events, people, places, objects or abstractions.

To help you get started, I've compiled my own list. Your own list should be much more comprehensive.

Buzz Words

Events:

- Christmas
- Wedding
- Birth
- New Year
- War
- Robbery
- Olympics
- Christening
- Easter

People:

- Surgeon
- Vicar
- Clown
- Dentist
- Gambler
- Racing Driver
- Supermodel
- Detective

Places:

- Zoo
- Airplane
- Palace
- Beach
- Ruins
- Bank vault
- Cathedral
- School
- Museum

Objects:

- Dagger
- Diamond
- Caviar
- Ice cream

- Rose
- Candle
- Treasure
- Rocking horse
- Mercedes

Emotions:

- Fury
- Passion
- Envy
- Desire
- Betrayal
- Pain
- Obsession
- Revenge
- Betrayal

Switch-Off Words

Once you've collected some buzz words, I'd like you to think about their opposites. At best, they have limited interest to the general public; at worst, they're likely to make a reader fall into an instant slumber.

Examples of these words or phrases might be: 'planning permission'; 'structural placement'; 'thermo-dynamics'; 'osmosis'; 'alliteration'; 'housing committee'; 'market averages'; 'capitalisation'; 'biomaterials'; 'environmental officer'; etc.

Yes, you may be yawning already. But you'd be surprised how many writers put these types of words in their synopsis or book blurb. Yes, really!

Exceptions To The Rule

The only exception to this rule is if you're writing a book for a niche market. In this case, you should know the type of keywords your target audience will respond to. A group of financial traders, for example, is likely to be interested in: "stop losses", "hedging" and "straddle orders"!

Similarly, English Literature students are likely to understand and relate to terms like: "onomatopoeia", "assonance", "alliteration" or "Hemingway-esque".

That said, bear in mind that if a literary agent starts to feel bored, they're unlikely to read your book.

If you want to break in to the world of mainstream publishing, then you need to choose words and write in a way that will appeal to a wide readership.

This can ultimately make the difference between a print run of 1000 and a print run of 100,000 or even 1,000,000!

Word Associations

Once you've collected a list of buzz words, re-examine them. Notice how your emotions switch in the blink of an eye as you glance down your list. Previous experiences and word associations come into play. Your imagination fills in the blanks. Each word prompts a different response.

For every person, these emotional associations – whether symbolic or otherwise – may be different. A person who fell off a rocking horse and broke their arm as a child, is likely to have a very different association to a person who happily day-dreamed of owning their own pony, for example.

However, there are certain buzz words that provoke a pretty universal response (such as champagne, roses or hearts). This, of course, is how companies make millions from seasonal events like Valentine's Day.

While it may feel a little manipulative or unnatural, this is something that's happening in the world around us every day. As we go about our business, we're continually being exposed to symbols and messages that give rise to powerful emotional responses.

Your aim is to harness this power in order to help sell your manuscript.

What Next?

Exercise One

i) Consider what type of buzz words you should use in your covering letter, your synopsis, and your opening chapters.

ii) If you've already written your covering letter, synopsis and opening chapters, are there any 'switch-off' words you can get rid of or replace?

iii) Have you got the balance right? (Note that a lightness of touch and subtlety is required. If you use too many buzz words, this can be just as off-putting.)

Chapter 8

Preparation Is Everything

Creating Anticipation

Remember that feeling you got as a child looking at the gifts under the Christmas tree?

Wasn't the build-up part of the thrill and excitement? Wasn't the anticipation just as much fun as opening the presents? And sometimes, weren't the colourful wrapping paper, the ribbons and the shiny baubles almost as exciting as the gifts themselves?

This is about suspense and tension. It is about fanfare. It is about setting up an expectation, purposefully delaying the gratification of it, then delivering something worth waiting for.

If you're clever, you can use this same principle to pique the interest of a literary agent or publisher before sending your manuscript to them. Build up a sense of anticipation with your submission letter. Tantalize with your synopsis. Engage their emotions or attempt to rouse their curiosity. If you can successfully connect with them, it's inevitable that they'll want to know more.

Entice Agents To Read Your Book

Your 'pitch' or 'submission package' – your covering letter, synopsis, author biography and sample chapters – are what you will use to entice agents and publishers to read your book.

Many writers find this task of condensing down information to its bare bones extraordinarily difficult and challenging. However, don't be daunted. You've already done most of the preparation for this. Now you're on the home straight!

To help you with this, I've put together various examples of notes for 'pitches' that I have worked on with clients. You can use these as your templates.

I should point out that you are compiling preliminary notes for your own benefit at this stage. This is NOT what you will send an agent or publisher.

Example One
A Non-Fiction Book To Help People Who Are Scared Of Flying

Readership:

Holidaymakers, business people and occasional travellers who are fearful of flying. 18+ years of mixed gender. NOT aimed at psychologists, academics, etc. – though they could recommend this to their clients.

Genre:

Self-help.

Selling Points:

Over 25 million Americans estimated to have a phobia of flying. Ties in well with summer holiday period. Airports and travel agents could provide point of sales. Written by a leading psychologist.

Buyers' Motivation:

Pain – solves a problem / fear.

Keywords:

Fear, flying, phobia, expert, help, holiday, travel, anxiety, worry, airplanes, airports, safety, panic attacks, psychology, self-help, hypnosis.

Example Two
A Novel About An Illicit Love Affair In Post-War Iran

Readership:

Predominantly women. Readers of literary fiction and romance.

Genre(s):

Literary fiction, women's fiction, cultural fiction, romance.

Selling Points:

Author lived in Iran – and is able to offer insights into a secretive regime. Illicit love affair. Insights into another culture usually veiled in secrecy: the morality police, floggings, virginity tests, torture, imprisonment, 'disappearances', war, bombings, etc. Growing interest in Islam and other cultures. Targeted at same readership as *The Kite Runner*, which at time of writing has sold eight million copies.

Buyers' Motivation:

Curiosity – intriguing subject matter and powerful plot.

Escapism – interest in a secretive culture.

Habit – will have bought similar books before.

Newsworthy – a topical subject that's in the news.

Keywords:

Illicit, forbidden, secret, torture, love affair, lies, subterfuge, floggings, disappearance, war, prison, imprisonment, virginity tests, Islam, bombing, Saddam Hussein, Iran.

Example Three
Non-Fiction Book: A Business Start-Up Guide For Gay Entrepreneurs

Readership:

Gay men and women thinking of quitting their job and starting a business. Gay men and women interested in wealth creation and entrepreneurialism.

Genre:

Business, Personal Finance.

Selling Points:

Specifically for gay men and women. Written by a self-made millionaire. A 'blueprint' for gay men and women who are struggling to make money from their business. Lots of case studies and examples. Problem-solving. Identifies top mistakes and pitfalls.

Buyers' Motivation:

Knowledge – up-to-date information about business start-ups.

Problem-solving – provides solutions.

Inspirational – provides role models and step-by-step solutions.

Keywords:

Gay, lesbian, blueprint, inspirational, business, entrepreneur, millionaire, millions, make money, cash, role model, mansion, sports car, holiday, yacht, luxury, start-up, opportunity, struggle, mistakes, pitfalls, prejudice.

Example Four
A Modern-Day Jewish Gangster Novel

Readership:

Men. Readers of crime / thriller / gangster novels.

Genre:

Crime. Gangster. Thriller.

Selling Points:

Action-packed plotline. An English 'Godfather'. Violence, guns, robberies, revenge, killings, betrayal, etc. An insight into a hidden underworld. Sex scenes. Complex father-son relationship.

Buyers' Motivation:

Escapism – insights into gangland murders and loyalties.

Excitement – longing to get away from the mundane and ordinary. Stories of daring and violence.

Habit – Readers will have bought similar books in the past.

Keywords:

Gangster, godfather, violence, robbery, danger, revenge, murder, guns, despair, friendship, gang, enemy, guns, sex, love, betrayal, loyalty, rival.

What Next?

Exercise One

Put together notes for your pitch as shown in the examples above.

Use the following categories:

i) Readership:

ii) Genre:

iii) Selling Points:

iv) Buyers' Motivation:

v) Keywords / Buzz Words

Chapter 9

The 'Must Have' Submission Letter

Your Letter Is Crucial

Not many writers realise this, but when approaching agents, your submission letter may actually be more important than your manuscript.

Yes, you heard that right. Annoyingly, in the publishing world, your one-page covering letter may open more doors for you than the 90,000 word book you lovingly crafted.

The standard 'pitch' or 'submission package' usually comprises of:

- a covering letter
- a synopsis (including endorsements / testimonials)
- an author biography
- sample chapter(s)

Now, here's the important bit. This is the EXACT same order in which literary agents read them.

They read your covering letter first. If your book appeals to them, they then read your synopsis and biography.

If they like these, they then move on to the sample chapter(s).

If the first page appeals, they read your opening chapter for as long as it excites or intrigues them.

If you keep them sufficiently interested to keep turning the pages, they will then ask to read your full manuscript.

This is a chain of events. Your letter is the FIRST link in this chain. If the agent isn't grabbed by your covering letter, then your synopsis and sample chapters are unlikely to be read.

Perhaps you can see now why it's VITAL to get your covering letter right!

Don't Bungle It

Publishers and literary agents receive all sorts of letters from writers desperate to get their work published. Unfortunately, in an effort to make an impression, it's all too easy to bungle the job.

I've seen plenty of examples over the years. They have included such gems as:

- *I'm offering you the chance of a lifetime.*
- *I need money as I've recently been made redundant.*
- *My novel is a literary masterpiece. My style is that of Salman Rushdie.*
- *Reject this book and I guarantee you'll regret it forever.*
- *This book is bound to be a Hollywood blockbuster.*

Yes, honestly – I'm not making these up! I'm all for being confident and believing in your writing; I'm also in favour of thinking BIG. However, agents like to make up their own minds, so sometimes it's best to keep these thoughts to yourself. The aim is to sound as impartial as possible.

The Golden Rules

When writing a covering letter, the rules are the same as those of simple social etiquette:

1. Avoid emotional blackmail

Don't use emotional blackmail – however subtle – by informing the recipient of your redundancy, illness, divorce, bereavement, etc.

If your book is about redundancy, illness, divorce, bereavement, etc. this is fine as it highlights your experience. Similarly, if you are writing a book to raise money for charity, this is relevant.

If not, leave out such information.

2. Don't drone on

Do not write a marathon-length hand-written letter. The last thing any agent wants is an essay about your book. Type your letter and keep it short. The shorter, the better! One double-spaced page is perfect.

3. Avoid sounding amateurish

Don't tell a publisher how great your book is. Don't tell them you have road-tested it on your friends and family. Don't tell them that your kids all love it. This just sounds unprofessional.

4. Avoid delusions of grandeur

Don't boast or compare yourself directly to a literary genius. There is a subtle difference between stating that you're aiming for the same target market as Alex Haley, and stating that you're a self-appointed candidate for the Pulitzer Prize.

5. Don't insult or threaten

Don't threaten or insult a publisher or agent, even in jest. Quite simply, they might not find such humour funny. And if you're serious, why would they want to work with someone who is trying to bully them?

6. Don't bore them

Make sure the information in your submission letter is *relevant*. Don't tell the literary agent that you've been married for 40 years, have 10 grandchildren and have a holiday home in the south of France unless this is relevant to your book.

The Ideal Submission Letter

1. One-Line Pitch

First and foremost, agents are looking for a brief description of your book and why it's likely to be of interest to them. For this, you will need a brief summary of your book.

This is generally referred to as a 'one-line pitch'. (There is a chapter devoted to this later in the programme.)

You are aiming for a tantalising or intriguing one-liner that gives a flavour of what your book is about.

2. Endorsement

If your book has received praise or an endorsement from a professional source – for example, from a published author, a journalist, a professional editor or a leading expert in your field - this will give you tremendous leverage.

There is a free report together with this home study programme that tells you *exactly* how to go about getting professional endorsements – and it's far easier than you might think.

Choose your best endorsement and use it in your covering letter.

3. Establish Your Credibility

If you're a professional in a field related to your book (eg. if you're a lawyer writing about crime, or a collector writing about gold coins) then state this, as it adds authority to your work.

If you have any experience that's informed your book, or if there's anything else that has a significant bearing on your writing, include this.

This should ideally be no more than a summary of one or two sentences.

4. Previous Published Work

If you've had work previously published or won writing competitions, this lends credibility to your submission. The same applies to creative writing courses you may have attended.

Again, keep this as brief as possible. Generalised phrases such as "won various literary competitions including XXX" or "published in various literary magazines including XXX" are preferable to long, blow-by-blow lists. Do *not* list every book and publication. Three names should suffice.

To help you, I'm including sample templates of submission letters I have written together with clients. Note that we took time to *personalise* the names rather than using the generic 'Dear Agent' or 'Dear Sir/Madam'.

You'll notice that we only used information that was RELEVANT. We also made the most of strengths – allowing slightly more page space to information that was especially attractive to agents.

Example One

Dear Agent

I am looking for an agent to represent my novel XXX based on a triple murder that took place in 1940.

XXX is a fictional account of a crime of passion that scandalised high society in the 1940s. An editor for The Oxford Literary Consultancy, who critiqued my book, has described this as: "a cracking story (made all the more fascinating by the fact that it's true). It's got mystery, suspense, intrigue, passion... In short, I loved it. I'm sure that it merits publication - and a wide audience... Indeed, the entire book's so good that I feel nervous even suggesting alterations, as I'd be loath to change much at all."

As a professional solicitor, I have had access to the original estate papers, family photographs and newspaper reports linked with this Old Bailey trial. I have represented clients in the Old

Bailey and Criminal Court of Appeal which have changed little since the original trial in 1940.

I am enclosing a synopsis for my novel. If you would like to read sample chapters, please let me know. I look forward to hearing from you.

Yours faithfully

Example Two

Dear Agent,

I'm looking for an agent to represent my book, X, which would suit the same target readership as Nadeem Aslam's best-selling books.

The book tells the story of a young teenager who leaves his wealthy Saudi family to become a jihad terrorist for al Quaeda - taking part in brutal killings, an assassination and eventually a suicide mission.

Like my character, I was recruited into the extreme Islamic movement, aged just 16, and saw action in Bosnia, Afghanistan and the Philippines. However, after a lot of soul-searching, I eventually left the jihad.

I am now writing under a pseudonym to protect my identity, though I would be willing to do media interviews to promote the book, if necessary. My intention is to inform and help other impressionable teenage boys.

I have attached a synopsis; if you would like to read sample chapters, do let me know.

I look forward to hearing from you.

Best wishes

Example Three

Dear Agent

I am looking for an agent to represent my children's book, XXX.

XXX is a quirky humorous book of short stories for 8 to 10-year-olds.

An editor at Oxford Literary Consultancy highlighted my book's commercial potential, saying it would fit well into the 'Horrible Histories' market: "This is a collection of short stories with a playful sense of fun and mischief... They are quirky and fun, and their 'gross' value is guaranteed to delight children in the target age range."

I am enclosing a synopsis and sample chapter for your consideration. If you would like to read more of the manuscript please let me know.

I look forward to hearing from you.

Best wishes

All the aforementioned letters hooked top literary agents in under a week. There was no need to send out dozens of submissions – or for that matter, to receive dozens of demoralizing rejections. Though the mischievous part of me thinks I should have added a not-so-good letter to let you guess the odd one out!

What Next?

Exercise One

i) Condense the synopsis of your book to two sentences or less. (You can find out more about the one-line pitch in Chapter Nineteen of this guide.)

ii) Jot down a list of professional qualifications or personal experiences that have helped when writing your book. Include previous publications or prizes if relevant. Summarise these in two sentences or less.

iii) What is your target readership and genre? Consider your book's unique selling points and any statistics that demonstrate potential readership – if relevant. Summarise this information in three sentences or less.

iv) Has your manuscript received a recommendation from a professional source such as an editor, novelist, journalist, expert, celebrity or thought leader? If so, condense the best quotation to around two sentences.

v) Write a draft of your submission letter, using the information from the previous exercises.

vi) Check your letter to see if there's anything non-essential that you can take out. Your letter will ideally be no longer than one page.

This means one page of double-spaced 12 point typeface.

Single spacing or smaller typeface is <u>cheating</u>!

Aim for an at-a-glance list of selling points.

Chapter 10
Selling Yourself

YOU Are Part Of Your Brand

Chances are you've never thought of yourself as a product before. If you're like the majority of writers, you've probably never considered what your own selling points are or what your personal sales pitch is.

While many writers accept the need to market their books, some have trouble getting to grips with the idea of selling themselves. Many writers I know are introspective or retiring. Others don't want to seem boastful or arrogant.

As a result, this area of book marketing is often over-looked.

Gently Does It

Promoting yourself does not have to be a lights blazing, trumpets blaring, all-singing, all-dancing affair. This approach is fine if you're outgoing in nature and it suits your temperament. However, marketing yourself can also be done in a subtle manner.

Writers often say to me: "I'm too old" or "I'm not good-looking enough" or "I don't have any literary connections". My answer to this is: "So?"

What matters most is your emotional connection with your readers. If you can speak to them with authenticity and passion in a way which stirs them, if you inspire them, move them to tears, or help them answer a problem in their lives, this is what will have the most impact.

Your Potted Biography

There are various aspects to marketing yourself. The first is your biography that will be sent out with your submission package. This can be used to emphasise your professionalism, your credentials, or your personality.

Your biography should be around 50 to 100 words and should be written in the third person. Publishers do NOT want to read your employment resume or know all your qualifications and achievements to date. They want an overview. The shorter, the better.

Your biography should contain brief details of any previously published work. If you've received tuition or mentoring from a published author, this is the ideal moment to mention it.

Your biography can also contain any experiences that formed the basis for your book. You can include anything else that has a significant bearing on your work.

Don't worry if you've already mentioned this information in your covering letter.

In marketing, the aim is to: tell them what you're going to tell them; then tell them; then tell them what you've just told them. This said, use different words each time to avoid being boring!

And prioritise. If you have too much information, you are going to have to decide which is the most eye-catching and relevant.

On the other hand, if you're feeling flummoxed and short of things to say, include some quirky facts about yourself.

Biographies are one area where it's acceptable to be a little playful. This is a good opportunity to show some warmth, to reveal a little of your personality, and to 'connect' with the agent or publisher.

To help you, I've provided some basic templates for simple author biographies.

Example One

XXX has been a professional stamp collector since the 1950s. He's had numerous articles published in The Collector and The Stamp Enthusiast.

His blog and newsletter have over 250,000 subscribers.

He regularly lectures on the subject and exhibits his stamp collections around the world.

This is a formal straightforward biography, which emphasises the writer's authority and credentials as he is writing for a niche market. It shows that he has knowledge of his subject area, and that he's written for national publications before. The reference to his mailing list implies a ready readership for his book on specialist stamps.

Example Two

XXX worked part-time in an ice cream parlour to research her book. She loves ice cream of all flavours, but her all-time favourite is Cherry Garcia.

She has attended several writing courses at The Arvon Foundation and has been mentored by award-winning author, Stephanie Hale, for the past 12 months.

This is a biography that balances the writer's literary credentials with a light-hearted approach. Information about her writing classes and mentoring shows that she has had formal teaching and is serious about her craft. Her employment in the ice cream parlour highlights the background research she has done for her novel. The personal information about her favourite ice cream gives a hint of fun. This suggests an amiable person who will be enjoyable to work with.

Example Three

XXX has wanted to write books since she was a child. She loves sports and always dreamed of finding a magic football. She has been a primary school teacher for the past 10 years. You can find her most Sundays standing on the side of a football pitch as she is referee to her under-11 team.

This is an informal autobiography that is in keeping with a book for children. It emphasises the playful side of the writer's life, while reinforcing her knowledge about both her subject matter and her target audience.

How Are You Coming Across?

There's another area to consider when you're selling yourself. You need to persuade a publisher or agent that you'll be a pleasure to work with. You must convince them that you're someone who delivers manuscripts on time; someone who aims for the highest possible standards; someone who is receptive to advice and criticism; and someone who will be reliable and considerate.

This can be shown through your actions and through respectful correspondence. Later on, when you finally meet your agent or publisher, it can be shown through your face-to-face dealings with them.

A Cautionary Tale

As a cautionary tale, let me mention a former client of mine who was intensely anxious about his work. One week he was in the pits of despair, believing he would never get published. The next week his emotions see-sawed and he had ideas for five other novels that he believed might be more marketable than his first. The author – who was very talented – was desperate to see his first novel in print.

The mistake he made was to put this desperation into action. Any editor who showed even a smidgeon of interest (and there were several) was then bombarded with email after email. Some of these missives were sent in the middle of the night after my client had had one vodka too many.

This author had written a novel on a subject that was highly 'fashionable' at the time, although it still needed minor tweaks to the plot. He looked as if he had everything going for him. However, his temperament was such that he was his own worst enemy. The publisher who wanted to print his novel eventually pulled out of the deal on a flimsy pretext. It wasn't hard to read between the lines.

Strictly Business

Many writers share similar anxieties about their work. However, they usually discuss them in more appropriate ways – with spouses, close friends and in writers' groups. Never confuse your personal and your professional life. No matter how friendly or interested an agent or publisher might seem, no matter how flattered you might be by their attentions, it is best to keep your relationship on strictly business terms.

It goes without saying you should never contact them after you've been drinking, taking recreational drugs or if you are feeling excessively angry or annoyed. Nor will they appreciate phone calls on weekends or evenings – especially to their mobiles, which they will most likely take home with them.

Several years ago, I was sitting in a literary agent's office in London after an inebriated (and prominent) author was mistakenly put through on the phone. The author in question was at the pinnacle of his career, so allowances were made. Afterwards, the agent sighed and told me with considerable irritation that his PA got such calls "once or twice a week". In this business, agents and publishers work many hours over and above what they are paid for, and such behaviour only serves to rub them up the wrong way.

Writing is your obsession. It's your passion. It has to be or you wouldn't make all the sacrifices necessary to complete a book. This is what pushes you on. It is your strength and your driving force. Channel this energy wisely. Use it. Never let it become your weakness!

What Next?

Exercise One

i) Make a list of all your professional qualifications and experiences to date. Is there anything that has any bearing on your book?

ii) Make a list of all your hobbies and interests. Is there anything that may intrigue or engage a publisher, or that lends weight to your book?

iii) Make a list of quirky things you do, be it collecting shoes or eavesdropping on the bus. Is there anything funny or heart-warming that other people will relate to?

Exercise Two

i) What sort of impression would you like your biography to give?

ii) In what ways will your biography help to sell your manuscript?

Exercise Three

Write an author biography of 50-100 words based on these notes.

Chapter 11
Write A Sensational Synopsis

Keep It Short And Simple

The long-winded synopsis is one of the most common errors that writers make.

Many authors mistakenly believe they should write a blow-by-blow account of every twist and turn of their book. As a result, I regularly see synopses that are 3-10 pages long. A synopsis like this is unlikely to do writers any favours at all.

Here's why. Imagine a huge pile of manuscripts sitting on an agent's desk when they get into work on Monday morning. They have phone calls to make, meetings to attend, emails to send, contracts to sign. Now, imagine how they'll feel if they open their post to find each writer has sent in a lengthy synopsis detailing their plot in microscopic detail?

Are they going to send a letter saying: "Yes please - send me more"? Or are they more likely to toss it on the slush pile for an office junior to deal with?

It's not that they're uninterested. It's not that they're not hungry for new talent or the next bestseller. It's just that they're overstretched and busy like the rest of us. Imagine an agent or publisher as a prospector searching for a gold nugget in a riverbed. They want this gold nugget. They really do. You just have to help them find it hidden under several tons of silt.

Avoid A Dull Synopsis

Your synopsis should not contain long lists of data, place

names, dates or statistics. It should not list the contents of every chapter. It should not give detailed technical analysis written in 'officialese' or jargon. Dull vocabulary should be avoided at all costs.

If you've written a novel, don't lay out your protagonists' background up to the present day. No one is really interested if Deirdre is Helen's cousin, or if she used to work in a store with Michael 20 years ago.

These things will achieve one thing and one thing only – they are guaranteed to make your an agent or publisher hurl your book into the abyss.

Write A Synopsis That Shines And Sparkles

A killer synopsis is usually written in everyday language that its target readers can relate to. It rarely gives a blow-by-blow account of a plot. Rather, it intrigues and tantalises.

Importantly, it is loaded with buzz words – words that trigger emotions and stimulate the imagination.

It gives a taste of a book and leaves the reader hungry for more.

Occasionally, I'm asked by writers whether it's okay for them to write one synopsis for an agent or publisher, and then revert back to their previous (duller) version when their book is published!

At this stage in the proceedings, I'm sure you can work out the answer to that question for yourself.

Anyone who has ever been warned that writing a book is just the beginning will now understand why. Once your book appears with your name emblazoned on the cover, you'll have the general public to convince. You don't want your book ending up in a remainder bin or being pulped to build sections of UK motorways!

While I'm in favour of recycling, this does seem rather a waste of authors' talents. Apparently, on some stretches of the M6 motorway, 4,500 books have been used for every mile of tarmac!

To help you, here are some samples of synopses that I've helped clients write over the years.

Example One
Pomegranate Sky – by Louise Soraya Black

Layla meets her boyfriend in secret, always afraid that she will be spotted by the komiteh, the morality police. This is Tehran, a city where unmarried couples risk a flogging, and partygoers face imprisonment or virginity tests if they are caught.

Layla has good reason to be wary. Her uncle, Massad, is a dissident journalist who has been tortured and imprisoned for his outspoken beliefs. When he dies alone on a snow-covered mountain top, a question mark hangs over his death.

Grieving over this loss, Layla breaks a cardinal law of the Islamic Republic. From here on, events take an unexpected turn and darker secrets begin to surface.

This is a gripping story of lies and subterfuge set against a backdrop of anti-regime protests in Iran. The beauty and exoticism of Tehran contrasts with the ever-present komiteh, and the terror caused by Saddam's bombings during the war.

The book is targeted at the same readership as The Kite Runner which sold eight million copies worldwide and has been translated into 40 languages.

Endorsements

"I was totally captivated by this novel. Layla is torn between her heart and the restrictions of her culture. She obeys her heart – though not without a price. This wonderfully poetic story keeps you hooked right to the very end."

Stephanie J. Hale, Director, Oxford Literary Consultancy

The Author

Louise Soraya Black lived in Iran during the Iran-Iraq war while her father ran a family hotel. Her time in Tehran made a huge impression on her.

Born to an English mother and Iranian father, she spent her first 17 years overseas. She lived in countries including Pakistan, Bangladesh and Indonesia.

Louise works as a corporate lawyer, based in London. Although her life is now based in the UK, she still visits her family in Tehran most summers.

Example Two
Too Gross? Too True! – by Sarah Loving

These stories are all true. And they could happen to you - though with luck they never will.

Because when you read them you'll find some pretty shocking things going on. Stomach-churning, toe-curling, disgusting things.

Just imagine:

- You're at breakfast. You take a slice of bread out of the packer. Something truly horrible falls on the breadboard. What's the worst thing it could be?

- A sheep dies after a long and happy life. What do her two best friends the pigs do? Do they bury her? Errr... not exactly...

- So you think boiled eggs are harmless? Really? Think again...

- Your toilet's out of order. You're desperate for a wee. What's the most revolting thing you could do next?

Are they gross? Are they funny? Will they make you squirm in disgust? Whatever you think of them, you wont want to put these stories down - if your parents will actually let you read them. And if you're not allowed to read them, they'll certainly be read by your parents when you're not around.

Recommendation

"This is a collection of short stories with a playful sense of fun and mischief. Children will love the risqué aspects of the collection... These are the stories, whispered behind hands, that parents would rather their children didn't know. They are quirky and fun, and their 'gross' value is guaranteed to delight children in the target age range."

Stephanie J. Hale, Director, Oxford Literary Consultancy

The Author

Sarah Loving (yes, that is her real name) lives in a house in Oxford, but would much rather she still lived on a boat. She spends her work time making maths fun for people. In her spare time she's crazy about creepy-crawlies of all kinds, which could explain why she's married to a stick insect. She's a terrible eavesdropper, so watch what you say on the bus.

Example Three
My Great Game – Following Francis Younghusband – by Tom Broadbent

My Great Game is the outstanding story of a solo 4,000-mile journey across Asia. Tom Broadbent does what many talk about but never actually do. Giving up his career as an auditor, he sets off on the road with £10 sponsorship in his pocket and little preparation beyond Tai Chi and macrobiotics.

In a journey fraught with danger, Tom escapes rape in the Karakoram tribal areas where Osama Bin Laden hides. He nearly dies in a riverbank landslide, survives dog bites and rabies injections, falls down one mountain pass and almost freezes on another.

In China, where social compliance is imperative, he walks through forbidden zones, bends rules, and battles with officials to gain insights into a country rarely glimpsed by outsiders. When placed under house arrest, he sits for days through a kangaroo court.

Tom is following in the footsteps of his forebear - soldier, explorer and spy, Sir Francis Younghusband who wrote a book about his travels. Tom takes this book to the same places exactly one hundred years later. Re-creating the journeys of his grandfather's cousin, Tom tells their stories in parallel.

Coincidences abound as the hundred years between their travels meld. Travelling on foot, bike, horse, camel and bike, the combination of their times is a story few can hope to match.

This is not just another travel book – part biography of one of the extraordinary figures from the days of Empire, part autobiography, it is a history and story of an incredible journey.

Recommendations

'A fascinating and entirely engaging portrait of China, it's the first in a quartet of books charting Broadbent's adventures and I'm eager to read the next installment.'

The Independent on Sunday (August 14 2005)

'Every armchair traveller will delight in Tom Broadbent's companionship from Peking to Pindi, every active traveller must pay homage to his achievement.'

Book Front Cover - Travel writer, Dervla Murphy

Less Is More

I hope you will see from reading these sample synopses that there are benefits to having a synopsis that cuts to the chase. The shorter the synopsis, the more energy and momentum it has.

A long-winded synopsis, that gives lots of detail about subplots, can seem cumbersome in contrast. The more words, the more narrative clutter. It is rather like being in a gallery stacked high with so many sculptures and paintings, that you are unable to appreciate any single work of art.

Once all the excess words are stripped away, the buzz words that are left are much more striking. The focus is sharper. The selling points are much more apparent.

Hooking An Agent Before Your Book Is Finished

One more point: it is possible – and sometimes desirable - to find a literary agent before you finish your book. In fact, you can do this even before you <u>start</u> writing your book.

This is usually done with non-fiction books. It is somewhat harder and less usual for a work of fiction.

A word of caution, before you jump in: I can think of a client who sold her novel on the basis of the first 50 pages. It was a highly marketable book with a powerful one-line pitch. She was a first-time author and she had the reassurance of a publishing deal with Penguin – in return for a £3,000 advance.

Her next novel had a weaker plot, and was less marketable, but this time she waited until the manuscript was finished to sell it. She received a £25,000 advance.

Reassurance, or a decent advance? Only you can decide.

What Next?

Exercise One

Visit your local book store or www.amazon.com. Take a look at the jacket blurbs for a variety of books on the bestseller list. Read the blurbs of at least 10 books from a similar genre to your own.

i) Which book blurbs work best? Why? What do you like about them?

ii) Which book blurbs work least? Why? What do you dislike about them?

iii) What lessons can you learn and apply to your own synopsis?

Exercise Two

Write two <u>different</u> synopses for your book using the notes you collected in earlier chapters. Each synopsis should be no longer than one page.

Be careful not to overdo your buzz words and selling points. Your synopsis should flow naturally rather than seeming contrived or strained.

Exercise Three

Use your friends or family members as Guinea-pigs.

i) Which synopsis would be most likely to make them buy your book – and why?

ii) What do they find less effective or less interesting about your synopses – and why?

Exercise Four

Draft a final synopsis based on the feedback you have received.

Chapter 12
Start With A Bang, Not A Whimper

Is Your Sample Chapter Strong Enough?

You've got this far. The agent likes your covering letter and synopsis. S/he's intrigued. You are <u>so</u> close now. Soon, s/he's going to be asking to see your full manuscript.

You can hear the envelope rattling through your letterbox. You can see it lying on the doormat. You can feel it in your hands. Hell, you can even smell it.

But get this. If you don't grab him/her with your opening sentence... if you don't capture his/her attention by the end of your first page... s/he may not even turn to your second.

Yes, you heard that right. NOTHING else will be read. Those sample chapters that you laboured with, agonised over and tenderly crafted, may not even be glanced at.

This is why you MUST start with a bang, not a whimper!

Your Golden Opportunity

If you're a glass half-empty kind of a person, you'll probably feel like tossing your manuscript on the barbeque right now and pouring lighter fuel over it. If you're a glass half-full kind of a person – which I assume you are or you wouldn't have stuck with me this far – then you'll realise how precious this information is and what a golden opportunity it opens up to you.

If you have this inside knowledge that thousands of other

writers aren't aware of (and aren't prepared to act upon) think what an edge this gives you. Just think how much you can improve your chances if you adjust your strategy accordingly.

Phenomenally – that's how much!

Your Opening Page

It seems outrageous to reject manuscripts without reading them properly. However, the rationale for this is simple. Many editors and agents are doing the work of three people. They're over-stretched and under-resourced. They couldn't possibly read all the manuscripts that land on their desks each day. So they filter and scan instead.

There is a commonly-held belief among editors and agents that you can tell a publishable manuscript from the opening page alone. There are the odd exceptions to this rule, but not many. If you doubt this, think of the time it takes most people to buy a home. You know pretty much as soon as you walk through the front door if it's for you, don't you?

For that matter, what do you do in a bookshop? You glance at the title and the jacket blurb. You then start reading the opening page. Either you can't put it down and want to keep turning the pages or you feel like it isn't for you. If it bores you, or doesn't resonate, what do you do?

Exactly.

Avoid A Slow Build-Up

By now, I hope you are twitching with excitement and anticipation. What can you do with this knowledge? How can it be used to your advantage?

Well, it means that it's no good having a slow start, with a cliff-hanger or a controversy at the end of your opening chapter. There's no point having an argument, a shock revelation, a death or a gunfight some 10 pages in.

It needs to be on the first page – or even in the opening sentence - so that your reader is smacked right between the eyes. You want them thinking: 'Wow - what happens next?'

This rule applies whether you are writing fiction or non-fiction; whether you are writing for a niche market or a widespread readership. It applies whether you are an unknown author launching your first book or a celebrity writer publishing your fourth or fifth. It's also relevant regardless of whether you're self-publishing your own book with a small print run, or if you have a bestseller translated into several languages.

Which Chapters To Send?

Most publishers and agents publish specific criteria for submissions on their websites. While these vary, industry standard tends to be 20 to 50 pages of your book.

Occasionally, writers will send *ad hoc* chapters from later in their book, as they feel these are more dramatic or exciting than their opening.

Frankly, this is bonkers! If the reader has to wait until page 65 or even page 165 for something to grab their interest, this sends out a very negative message indeed.

Any literary agent worth their salt is going to be thinking: 'So what's wrong with the opening then?'

Consecutive chapters running from page one onwards are always going to be best for sample material. And if they're not your best pages, then you need to DO something about it.

Successful Opening Lines

To give an idea of what you're aiming for, let's take a quick look at some opening lines from successful books. I've deliberately chosen household names to show you that even celebrity writers employ these techniques:

Lyra and her daemon moved through the darkening Hall, taking care to keep to one side, out of sight of the kitchen.

Northern Lights – Philip Pullman

The key words here are 'daemon', 'darkening' and 'out of sight'. Our curiosity is aroused. What is a daemon? Why does Lyra want to keep out of sight? Why does she need to be so furtive? Who is she avoiding? Is she in danger? Will she succeed? The growing darkness enhances the mystery of what might be lurking in the shadows.

You are about to become rich. I don't care what your current financial situation is, what obstacles you might be facing or what challenges you have had to deal with in the past.

I Can Make You Rich – Paul McKenna

The confident assertion of the opening sentence speaks for itself. It suggests that if you read this book and follow all the advice, the results will follow automatically. Any reservations or problems the person has, are tackled in the second line. This is classic 'I have a problem, this product will fix it' marketing.

Cooking has many functions, and only one of them is about feeding people.

Feast - Nigella Lawson

A book about cooking that isn't about feeding people! This little conundrum is likely to have the reader sitting up and taking notice. At a deeper level, this is aspirational marketing based around food (and social) snobbery.

To summarise, these opening lines are like electric shocks that jolt the reader. They set up challenges. They make controversial statements. They rouse curiosity. They give the reader a good shake as if to say: "Stop whatever you're doing now and pay attention!"

Have you noticed that they also contain buzz words or selling points? Funny isn't it, how these marketing techniques keep cropping up? For what is an opening line, if not a teaser for your book? What is a first page, if not a blazing advert for your writing? This is your opportunity to pull on your readers' heartstrings, to offer them a message of courage or hope, to promise them inspiration and escapism.

Many writers don't realise this. Or they don't want to face the enormous task of rewriting their opening. However, ignore this fundamental rule, and you're unlikely to find an agent.

Yes, this may mean extra work... and frankly, it's a pain. But remember those goals you set yourself back in Chapter One? This is going to help you achieve them.

The best way to perceive this, is as an opportunity rather than a hurdle. Don't let it pass you by. Grab it with both hands. Embrace the challenge.

Great Opening Lines

Opening lines will ideally be any one of the following:

- Startling
- Unexpected
- Emotive
- Tantalising
- Humorous
- Bizarre
- Anarchic
- Subversive
- Unconventional
- Tense
- Dramatic
- Quirky
- Gripping
- Haunting
- Thought-provoking
- Challenging
- Daring

Now is NOT – most definitely not - the time to be worrying about 'showing off' or using attention-grabbing prose.

Twelve seconds! Write this on a large sheet of paper and stick it above your computer. This is how long you have to convince the average person to buy your book. If it takes longer than this to get your selling points across, you need to rewrite!

Do Your Chapters Need A Re-shuffle?

Re-examine your book. Could it be that Chapter 20 is really your Chapter 1? Or is there a paragraph in Chapter 3 that can be moved to the opening page?

Often I find that the opening of Chapter 1 starts several pages in. Or that the chapter can be fixed by flipping it head over heels – inserting the beginning at the end, and vice versa. Getting this right requires flexibility and creative thinking.

Some writers are fairly rigid in their ways and resist this suggestion. They do themselves and their book a great disservice as a result. I'm not suggesting that you just 'stick on' an eye-catching chunk of material just to arouse attention. There has to be fluidity and the events have to arise organically from the book's whole. No integrity should be lost.

It's Worth The Effort

If you get the formula right, you'll soon have dozens of letters requesting your full manuscript. I've seen this time and again with writers I've personally mentored. So don't give up, no matter how many rejections you've had before. Success may soon be within your grasp! This is your goal and your incentive.

Think now beyond your first line and page, to your entire opening chapter. How can this be improved? To help you, I've compiled my own list of what are generally considered to be qualities of strong and weak openings. Any one of these qualities is applicable regardless of whether you have written fiction or non-fiction.

Qualities of a Strong Opening

- *Intrigues the reader.*
- *Gives a clear indication of the mood and style of the book.*

- *Draws the reader in - by setting a challenge or by appealing to their emotions.*
- *Focuses on a dramatic moment, crisis or trigger point.*
- *Introduces a central conflict or hurdle.*
- *Provokes questions.*
- *Makes a controversial statement or assertion.*
- *Provokes an emotional response – laughter, sadness, shock, horror, anxiety, wonder, or curiosity.*
- *Drip-feeds information rather than over–explaining background and history.*

Qualities of a Weak Opening

- *Used as a curriculum vitae for protagonists and characters.*
- *Burdened with dull exposition or trivial detail.*
- *Contrived, stilted or clichéd.*
- *Introduces too many people, places, events, dates.*
- *Has a slow build-up and takes too long to get started.*
- *Written in a dull style that feels 'flat' and monotonous.*
- *Over-wordy or cluttered with adjectives and adverbs.*
- *Uses inappropriate language for the target reader.*

What About The Classics?

There will always be quick-witted clients who point out that many classic books have slow or over-wordy openings.

Books by some of the world's most acclaimed authors possess

many of the qualities mentioned under the latter list. Novels by authors such as Daniel Defoe, Henry James, George Eliot or Herman Melville are good examples.

However, times have changed. As society has evolved – particularly with the development of film, television and the Internet – we have become a population seeking instant gratification.

We want drama and entertainment and don't want to wait for it. If something bores us, it can be switched off at the click of a button. Or we flick channels and replace it with something else.

We are uncompromising in our desire to be entertained. We want excitement and thrills, and we want them *now*!

Every book throughout history is a unique event within its own lifetime. It tells us something about an era and its people - about their values and expectations. It's a sad fact that many classics published in the past wouldn't stand a ghost of a chance today.

Today provides you with your chance to celebrate your own special place in history. Your prose is alive, vital and energetic. After all your hard work, your manuscript is about to assume a life of its own and weave its own magic.

By writing a book, you've already achieved something that over 80 per cent of people dream of, but very few achieve.

It's therefore worth this extra effort to get it right so that others can share your vision.

What Next?

It's important to start with a clean slate here. If you've already written an opening, put it to one side for now.

Exercise One

i) Make a list of openings in books that have hooked you in.

ii) Make a list of openings that you consider to be dull or boring.

iii) Identify the qualities that make you want to read on or buy a book.

iv) Identify the qualities that make you want to stop reading or doze off.

Exercise Two

i) Think about a conflict or controversy that stands out in your book. Make a list of any dramatic scenes or intriguing moments (both fiction and non-fiction).

ii) Would any of these make an attention-grabbing opening for your book?

Exercise Three

Think about your opening line.

i) Is there an intriguing phrase or event that can be used in your first sentence? Can you open with a challenge? Is there something dramatic or controversial you can use?

ii) Write 10 alternative opening lines. Make each one as different as possible.

Exercise Four

i) How can you make your opening chapter more attention-grabbing? Can you switch around some of your existing chapters? Can you tweak the chapter you already have, or do you need a complete rewrite?

Exercise Five

There's nothing for it. Roll your sleeves up and get down to it. Rewrite your opening page and chapter. (Yes, you can fill this space below with swear words if you like.)

Exercise Six

Give yourself a reward or treat. Buy a bottle of bubbly and organise a nice picnic. Go for a bike ride in the country. Book tickets for the cinema or theatre.

You've earned it!

Chapter 13
Spit and Polish

Getting Your Manuscript Ready

As mentioned earlier, my intention isn't to tell you how to write a publishable book. I'm trying to help you prepare the ideal submission package, assuming that you've already written a marketable manuscript.

However, my editor and Guinea-pigs (yes, I have them too!) suggested that I include a checklist for those of you who would like to tweak and revise your entire manuscript.

A common mistake with revision is to get bogged down with detail. Writers worry if a comma should be a semi-colon, if a dash should be a colon, or if they should lose three words from a sentence. They'd be better off wondering if their protagonist is mesmerising and if their ending packs a strong enough punch.

Though language is important, agents find it easier to forgive poor punctuation and weak sentence structure than an ill thought-through plot or an unbelievable protagonist. Plot and storyline are therefore where your main focus should be.

Your ability to write a gripping book is what will sell it, not the brilliance of your grammar. Writing a book is like building a house. There's no point glossing the skirting boards if there are bricks missing and the walls are higgledy-piggledy!

Confession time here. In days of yore, when Amstrad word processors were all the rage I wrote a novel, proudly printed it out, and sent it to a top literary agent. What I didn't realize was that the last line of every page – you read that right, *every* page – was missing. He read through my manuscript (with approximately 12 words of every 350 missing) saw the potential and *still* took me on. I tell you this anecdote both to reassure you that 'doh!' moments happen to all of us, and to illustrate where an agent's focus lies. If a plot is strong enough, 'technical hitches' – even bad ones – can be overlooked.

As mentioned before, there are more than enough 'Write a Bestseller' classes and books available, so I'll keep this editing checklist brief. I don't want to cover old ground if you've done your research already.

As far as possible, I've tried to include attributes that are applicable to both fiction and non-fiction.

Checklist

Human Interest

- Are there enough twists and turns in your book to captivate a reader? Do you have sufficient hurdles, challenges, controversies, hooks or questions?

- Is your book compelling and engaging? Is the plot fresh and lively, rather than predictable and boring?

- Do you use tension, suspense, or mini cliff-hangers, to heighten the drama?

- Is there sufficient intellectual involvement, allowing the reader to recognise universal truths and connections with their own lives?

Language

- Is your language appropriate to your target audience?

- Are your verb tenses consistent throughout? Have you checked that you haven't unintentionally switched from past to present tense or vice versa? (Although this can be used as a stylistic device, it should be used sparingly.)

- Have you considered whether generic or specific words are more appropriate. Generics (eg. meal, car, flowers) help avoid cluttering a narrative. Specifics (Chicken Chasseur, Skoda, snowdrops) are much more vivid.

- Have you avoided long and complex sentences, full of subordinate clauses that are overloaded with punctuation? A more direct style has greater impact.

Structure

- Is there a logical sequence to your book? Is it structured in a clear way?

- Is there a clear, understandable and plausible conclusion? Do you resolve conflicts, questions or predicaments?

- Is it obvious what the main driving force of your plot is?

- Is it obvious who your main protagonist is?

- Is your book a chain of: actions and reactions; questions and answers; hurdles and triumphs; failures and successes?

Continuity

- Is there consistency of time sequence, physical traits, weather, seasons, flora and fauna, ages, etc?
- Are flashbacks and time transitions clearly signposted?
- Is anything too vague or cryptic? Does anything need clarifying? Are changes in time or character clearly signposted? Does the reader always know whose point of view is being used?

Characters

- In a novel, are your characters multi-dimensional and well developed?
- Are your characters fascinating and believable (as opposed to realistic)?
- Do your characters have strong and consistent motivations?
- Can the reader empathise with them?

Cast

- Is your cast too large? Do you have too many minor characters?
- Can you lose anyone who takes the focus off the main characters?

Dialogue

- Is dialogue used to add an electric charge to your story

and bring characters to life?

- Is your dialogue convincing and believable, (rather than realistic, which is dull)?
- Do your characters all talk in a clearly differentiated way?
- Is your dialogue used to convey drama, further the plot, or aid characterisation?
- Have you avoided letting characters witter on, giving mundane information?

Pace

- Is there a strong sense of narrative momentum?
- Is your pace varied? Have you avoided your writing being either relentlessly plodding or perpetually frenetic?
- Does the book 'speed up' and 'slow down' in the right places? Think of your reader like a visitor on a tourist bus. The bus should slow down and linger at the points of interest, but speed by duller areas.

Editing

- Have you pruned out unnecessary words or phrases? Have you avoided using three words instead of one?
- Have you deleted adjectives and adverbs that slow down the pace?
- Have you trimmed long passages of exposition and description?
- Have you avoided tautology (saying the same thing twice

in different words).

Dramatisation

- Have you dramatised events where possible, using anecdotes or speech?
- Have you used the 'show, don't tell' principle?
- Have you avoided making bald statements telling the reader how knowledgeable, afraid, miserable or happy you or your characters are?
- Have you shown behaviour in an objective way, and allowed your readers to draw their own conclusions?

Symbolism And Imagery

- Are metaphors, similes and symbols used appropriately?
- Are they used in an original, rather than a clichéd way?
- Do they add sophistication and depth to your book?
- Do they help bring abstract ideas to life?

Accuracy

- Is your research up to scratch?
- Are language, events, costumes, behaviour etc. consistent with era and location.
- Do you need to contact someone with expert knowledge or do any further research?

Title

- Is your book title memorable enough?
- Does your book title contain a keyword or keywords?
- Is it intriguing?
- Does it convey what your book is about?

Attitude

- Are you in the right frame of mind while you're revising your manuscript?
- Are you editing while you're feeling positive and upbeat?
- Moods can distort your perception. If you edit while you're feeling tired or down, you may have to retrieve a lot of pages from your recycling bin later on!

Chapter 14

First Impressions

How To Present Your Manuscript

First impressions count. When someone walks into a room, we instantly form an opinion based on their appearance and demeanor before they even speak a word. Imagine someone attending an office interview with crusted gravy on their suit or wearing painting overalls. Hardly likely to get the meeting off on the right footing, is it? The same is true of manuscripts. An impression is formed in one glance.

Let's suppose I am a literary agent or publisher. I let authors know what I expect by publishing a brief outline in resources such as *The Writers' & Artists' Yearbook*. I put this same information on my website, stating clearly what I am looking for. What am I likely to think when I receive something that is the opposite?

How To Annoy An Agent

There is a standard presentation expected in the publishing industry. Agents don't want single-spaced pages, in tiny typeface that hurts their eyes. They don't want fancy headlines, funny gimmicks, or lurid-coloured paper. They don't want amateur-bound books, title pages with clip art, or your best friend's designs for a front cover.

Some authors send manuscripts that are riddled with spelling mistakes and typos. They neglect to number the pages. Or their work is single-spaced in miniscule 10-point typeface. I'm sure they think it's saving them a packet on printing and postage costs, but can you imagine how hacked off this makes literary agents?

In an age when most computers have spell-checkers and grammar-checking facilities, there's no excuse for sloppiness. I recommend buying a copy of the bestseller *Eats, Shoots and Leaves* by Lynne Truss to help you with this. Or alternatively, hire a proof-reader.

If you think clever gimmicks or tricksy typefaces will get you noticed, think again. It will make you stand out - but for all the wrong reasons. Stick with something safe like Times New Roman, Courier or Helvetica. Pages should be printed on one side in standard 12-point font. This should be aligned to the left with pages numbered.

OK, it's not massively original, but there are good reasons for this standardised presentation. It works! It's easier on the eye. There's space for editors to make notes in the margin. No pages get lost if the manuscript gets dropped on the floor.

The impression you want to give is of someone who is serious about their craft, who has done their research, and who will deliver high-quality work.

While 'industry standard' may seem a bit pedestrian or inflexible, there's nothing to be gained by breaking the rules. Yes, you want to get your manuscript noticed. However, there are more sophisticated and persuasive methods for doing this.

To help you, I've compiled a checklist of how your manuscript should be presented. You can run through this before sending out your submission package.

Checklist

Paper

Paper should be standard white A4 universal size. It should not be heavy expensive paper nor so flimsy that it tears easily.

Typeface

Use Helvetica, Times New Roman or Courier in 12 point.

Margins

Leave a 2.5cm margin on the left and right of each page. This enables agents and editors to make comments and amendments on the edge of your manuscript.

Format

All pages should be double-spaced and printed on one side only.

Again, this leaves space for notes and amendments.

If you don't know what double-spacing is or where to find it on your keyboard, then ask someone who does.

Pages

All pages should be numbered. Many agents and publishers take manuscripts home with them. It's a logistical nightmare when papers splay out and become separated, as often happens when reading a loose-leaf manuscript.

All pages should have either your name or the book title on them.

Align pages to one side. Do not justify the pages as this can make your manuscript look odd.

We've all seen examples of words that are unnaturally s t r e t c h e d as a result of justifying pages. Don't do it!

Chapters

Each chapter should start on a fresh page, rather than halfway down another one.

The reason for this is simple. There are occasions when chapters need rejigging in a book. Your Chapter 1 may in fact work better as Chapter 3. Or your Chapter 20 may be better as Chapter 2.

Having clear divisions between chapters allows for a substantial reshuffling of a manuscript.

Presentation

Manuscripts should be presented loose-leaf. There is a great temptation to staple it, clip it, or hole-punch it. However, resist doing this.

Do not date your work – if it has been doing the rounds for some time, this will be a bit of a give-away!

Often, the best solution to loose-leaf manuscripts is to put them inside a smart cardboard/plastic folder.

Cover Page

All manuscripts should have a cover page. This should include the title of your work, your name, your address, your phone number, your email address and a word count.

The word-count is essential. If there is no word-count function on your computer (which is highly unusual), then you can calculate word-count by finding the average words per page (usually around 325) and multiplying this by the number of pages in your manuscript.

Books tend to be published to a standard format based on profit margins. As a result, it's difficult for a book over 120,000 words to be printed because of the high production costs.

Publishers of adult novels tend to look for manuscripts of approximately 75-90 thousand words. Children's novels (for confident readers) tend to be around 30-40 thousand words. Picture books for toddlers are usually under 1000 words. Don't worry too much about running slightly over or under these limits.

Returned Manuscripts

Ensure that your manuscript always looks as crisp and clean as when it was first printed.

If your manuscript is returned after being sent out to agents or publishers, freshen up the pages. If the front cover looks dog-eared, or there are fingerprints or coffee stains on any of the pages, print them again.

No one wants to feel second-best or that they are looking at a manuscript someone else has rejected.

Using A Pseudonym

If you are using a pseudonym, print both names on the coversheet of your manuscript. You may choose a *nom de plume* if you wish to hide your identity or build a new readership. Mary Ann Evans wrote under the pen name George

Eliot, for example, to hide her gender. Stephen King used the alter ego, Richard Bachman, purportedly to prove his writing could succeed without his name on the book cover.

Think hard though before assuming another identity. It may be an advantage if you're a mid-list author re-launching your career or if you are writing books in two entirely different genres.

However, if you're a first-time author, your name can sometimes be a significant weapon in your marketing arsenal. How many acquaintances, friends, colleagues, and family do you have? How many lives have you touched? How many strangers have you met over the years? How many of these people are likely to buy your book, even out of curiosity?

Chapter 15
Who To Send To

Avoid The Spray-Gun Effect

The 'lazy' way to send out your manuscript is to post it willy-nilly to every publisher and agent you can get an address for. This is the spray-gun effect. If you're lucky, your book will hit its target. This is great if you want your 'chick lit' novel to end up with an agent specialising in historical sagas, or your book on World War Two sent to a sci-fi publisher. Not.

By now, you'll know that successful writers don't do lazy – they do research! Unfortunately, there is no quick and easy way to hit the jackpot other than through determination and hard work. It's a pain, I know. But hey, that's what separates the winners from the losers.

Ignore everything you read in the media. Genuine stories of "instant fame" and "meteoric success" are few and far between.

Many of the big names in writing have served long apprenticeships before achieving fame and fortune. Joanna Trollope must have had steam coming out of her ears when she told a journalist that it had taken her 20 years to become an overnight sensation. Author Philip Pullman, CBE, echoed the sentiment when he told a BBC reporter: "It took me 30 years to become an overnight success." Similarly, Mark Haddon was a writer and illustrator for 16 years before *The Curious Incident of the Dog in the Night-Time* won the Whitbread Award in 2003. His five attempts at writing an adult novel are apparently still languishing in a drawer.

Unfortunately, 'Shoots to Fame after Years of Hard Slog' does not make an appealing headline!

This is not to say that it will take you decades to hook an agent or get your book published. By no means! It took the aforementioned writers this long to achieve international success, Hollywood blockbusters, bestseller status, the Whitbread and a CBE.

Your own apprenticeship is already well underway. If you've done all the exercises properly, you'll have accelerated your progress in leaps and bounds.

Research Your Agents

You'll need to set aside at least half a day to research your target agents and publishers.

Reference guides such as *The Writers' & Artists' Yearbook* or *The Guide to Literary Agents* are a good starting point to identify lists of prominent agents and publishers around the world.

An up-to-date book is best to make sure you're not writing to someone who left the company three years previously or to an agency that has moved premises in the last 12 months. A second-hand book from 2006 is only going to lead to mistakes and trip you up.

Both books have convenient subject indexes at the back to help you locate your required genre. However, do not rely upon this alone. It is still best to check through individual entries. An agent with an entry that states "nurtures new talent" or "receptive to first-time authors", may not be in the index under your particular genre. However, this may be precisely the person that you need to send to. Similarly, an entry stating "accepts genre fiction of all types" or "represents commercial non-fiction" is not specific enough to be indexed.

Information for each agent and publisher varies widely. Some entries will give a list of all their current clients – in which case, you have to consider if the authors write similar books to your own. Other listings give specific genres that they would like to receive. Some will even state what they are <u>not</u> interested in.

A great resource for the American market is: www.publishersmarketplace.com.

This industry newsletter announces which books have been sold to which presses as well as which literary agent arranged the deal. Read the listings and take note when a book sounds similar to yours. You can also access the online database of agents and editors for a small fee.

If the handbook is your own, it can help greatly to use highlighter pens to mark up agents or publishers of particular note. You can colour code these using a 'traffic-light' system. Green for an A-rating, amber for B-rating, and red (or pink) for a C.

Acknowledgements

Many authors credit or thank their agents in the *Acknowledgements* section of their books. So if you can think of books similar to yours, this is a relatively easy (if time-consuming) way to discover the most likely targets for your manuscript. Simply go to a book store and jot down anything that seems promising in your particular genre.

You can also check out agents' and publishers' websites. If you want to earn extra Brownie points, identify the person most likely to be interested in your book and use their name. If necessary, phone to check. It's always best to use a name where possible. However, if after researching you still have no name, then address your letter to "Dear Sir/Madam" to avoid offence.

Remember The 'Gatekeepers'

Try not to overlook junior staff in addition to the established names. Those who have been kicking around for a while are likely to have full lists, whereas newer staff may be hungrier for fresh talent. If you can, get the names of their assistants too – PAs, secretaries, receptionists - they are the gatekeepers for these people. Be nice to them!

Check House Style

Check for house style and any specific requirements. Some will ask for one chapter, others for three chapters. If they ask for return postage or an SAE, then include them. If they ask for postal submissions only, then there's little point in sending a manuscript via email.

If a publisher states that they'll only accept work submitted by a literary agent or a literary consultancy (as many major publishing houses do), then respect this. If they ask for twenty sample pages only, don't send them fifty!

Make A Shortlist

Make a shortlist of your most suitable targets in priority order. If you have the facility on your computer, you might want to type up a list of labels for them. You can then work down your list, starting with the 'top priority' submissions first.

When you are ready to send your submission package out, compile an information sheet for each agent or publisher that you're sending to. Keep detailed notes so that you can keep track of your submissions. These notes can be updated as you send and receive correspondence.

Your completed information sheet may eventually look something like this:

Submission Sheet

Agent:	A.N. Agent
Literary Agency:	Curtis Brown Ltd
Address:	Haymarket House, 28/29 Haymarket London SW1Y 4SP.
Submission Date:	12 March
Sample Chapter:	Requested on 4 April. Sent Chapters 1-3.
Full MS:	Requested on 20 April. Sent full MS.
Response:	TBC

After following these steps, you should have a list of targets for your submission. This means that when you fire, your shot will be as precise as you can make it.

What Next?

- Draw up a list of potential agents or publishers using a 'traffic light' system.

- List them in descending order of preference, with your preferred agents and publishers at the top and your least preferred at the bottom.

- Identify the best person for your manuscript. Does the agency or publisher have an allocated script reader? Or is there someone in charge of your particular genre?

- Check house style and any special requirements. Do they ask for an SAE?

- Do they ask for email submissions only? Do they request sample chapters or for a synopsis only in the first instance?

- Purchase all the necessary stationery in advance as you may have a lot of printing to do. You'll find it cheaper to buy paper, envelopes and ink in bulk.

- I'd also suggest weighing one sample submission package and buying sheets of stamps in advance. This is a much better alternative to repeatedly queuing in your local post office.

- Create a template for your submission sheets. Print or Xerox a bundle of these, and keep them in a dedicated folder. Fill them in as and when you send out your submissions. Keep these records accurate and up-to-date.

- Relax. The majority of the hard work is done!

Chapter 16

Publishing Etiquette

How Many Submissions?

I'm going to stick my neck out here. Protocol dictates that you send out letters to no more than one agent or publisher at a time. This is the usual (and recommended) etiquette.

However, it's dog eat dog in publishing right now. So my advice is simple and straightforward. Do whatever it takes. If it means contacting every publisher and every agent you've targeted as suitable, then so be it. Send out six at a time. Send out 12 submission letters if necessary. Do you research, then put your sales pitch in an envelope, and get it out there.

All Power To You

If 12 agents get back to you, each of them wanting your book, then all power to you. Meet them all and choose the one you like best. Writers have many odds stacked against them these days. So I'm in favour of loading your canons with all the ammunition you can lay your hands on. When the target keeps moving or disappearing behind mist, you're going to need as many shots as you can get.

Rumour has it that you can't get a publisher without an agent, and that you can't get an agent without first getting published. Many agents and publishers state that they don't read unsolicited manuscripts, further perpetuating this myth.

In reality, if a pitch is enticing enough, most publishers or agents will look at it!

100 Submissions At A Time?

Writers sometimes ask me if they should post 100 submission letters to 100 agents all on the same week. Well, I applaud your enthusiasm, if you're also thinking like this. However, this isn't a route I'd recommend as it doesn't leave you much room for manoeuvre.

After all, if you've done the job properly, you should be getting several agents asking to see your manuscript right from the get-go. Do you really want to print that many copies of your manuscript all at once? Do you really want to have meetings with that many literary agents?

On the other hand, if you're <u>not</u> hooking agents at this early stage, then this provides you with valuable feedback. Perhaps your submission isn't as strong as you thought it was and it needs rewriting.

Similarly, if three agents read your sample chapters but say your cast is too large or that your heroine isn't feisty enough, this enables you to make adjustments.

Do all this all at once with 100 agents, and you'll give yourself with a headache. You'll also have had all your bites at the cherry all at the same time.

The 'Indies'

There are literally hundreds of publishers around the world.

These include the major global publishing conglomerates that are household names such as Simon & Schuster, Random House and HarperCollins. These excel in selling mass-market titles and have a world-wide reach.

However, the last 50 years have seen the birth of many new independent publishers that are prepared to take risks with new talent. The Independent Publishers Guild lists 480 companies in the UK alone – an all-time high – with a combined turnover of £500 million per year. These are small, independently owned publishing houses.

It is often said that small independent publishers – the 'Indies' - are powerhouses of innovation and new talent. Though the advances may be smaller, they are excellent at nurturing the careers of new authors. One only has to consider the successes of Yann Martel (Canongate), Alexander McCall Smith (Polygon Edinburgh) and Lynne Truss (Profile) to appreciate their enormous potential. Their main disadvantage is their smaller distribution and reach.

Over 25 per cent of the Top 100 bestselling Kindle books are from indie publishers according to retail data in 2013. There is no reason why one of these books should not be yours!

Timing Your Submission

Remember that if you submit your manuscript in the period from March to April or from September to October, responses may take longer as these are peak periods for sales conferences, holidays and book fairs.

Similarly, you can expect slower responses in the run-up to major holiday periods such as Christmas or Easter.

What Do Agents REALLY Mean?

Authors are frequently confused by what literary agents actually MEAN – especially if your manuscript has been read but has then been rejected. If an agents says you write well and that they enjoyed your book, you may wonder if you're just being fobbed off.

You're left wondering: 'Does this agent *really* like my book? Do they hate it? Have they read it at all?' You're left to make your own judgment how to interpret the rejection - and nine times out of ten, writers get this wrong. To take some of the guesswork away, I'll give a quick run-through of what agents' letters might say and what they most likely mean.

1. "We regret we're unable to take on any new writers."

Exactly that. Have they read your pitch? Probably not.

2. "Your synopsis and opening chapter have promise, but we already have a similar author on our list."

They can see the potential in your work. However, they are already representing a similar writer. They probably feel indifferent – no strong feelings one way or the other.

3. "I enjoyed reading your full MS. I just don't feel passionate enough about it to represent you."

Agents and publishers are rushed off their feet. They don't read manuscripts unless they seem marketable. The fact that they took time out of their busy schedule to read your work is an enormous compliment. They don't hand out praise lightly. They thought your work was good, but it was just missing that *X Factor* for them.

4. "The plot wasn't compelling enough. The narrative was plodding."

Time for a rewrite. Or a second opinion!

5. "This one's not quite right for me. But do send me your next book."

They can see your talent and promise. This particular book just isn't quite to their taste.

6. "I was sorely tempted by this."

High praise indeed. You were within a hair's breadth of hooking them. But something else got in the way – maybe work overload, maybe another contract. Infuriating I know. But let's focus on the positives here. It's worth contacting them again in future, perhaps with your next book idea.

7. "I'd like to meet you to discuss this further"

Bingo. They want to meet you to discuss possible representation. At this stage, they may still ask you for a rewrite of your book. Or they may want to know about your plans for future books. It's time to prepare for your big meeting!

Chapter 17

Rotten Rejections

Famous Rejections

I LOVE famous rejections… all the more so because the critics have been proved so utterly wrong. Tales of literary rejection are the stuff of myth and legend. So consider a handful of these tales and take heart:

- When H.G. Wells submitted *The Time Machine*, he was told: "It's not interesting enough for the general reader and isn't thorough enough for the scientific writer."

- Agatha Christie was rejected many times. Her first publisher, Bodley Head, sat on her book for 18 months before agreeing to publish it. She went on to write a further 90 titles.

- *Harry Potter and The Philosopher's Stone* was rejected by 12 publishers before finally being accepted. J.K. Rowling has since sold 325 million books in just under ten years!

- Iain Banks wrote five novels without success before his bestseller, *The Wasp Factory*, was retrieved from the slush pile at Macmillan.

- William Golding's *Lord of the Flies* received 21 rejections, before Faber & Faber spotted its potential.

- Beatrix Potter decided to self-publish her book after rejections from six publishers. She printed 250 copies of her Peter Rabbit books against the advice of publisher, Frederick Warne. Their popularity was such that he eventually agreed to launch the books, complete with coloured illustrations.

- After many rejections, Louisa May Alcott was advised: "Stick to your teaching; you can't write." Twenty years after self-publishing her first book of poetry, she was a bestselling author following the success of *Little Women*.

- "We're not normally this frank. But when someone has no idea of plot construction, characterisation, or narrative drive, we feel it's appropriate to advise you to rethink your career plans." Early advice for the late David Gemmell – bestselling British author of over 30 novels.

Mind Over Matter

We might think logically that we can cope with rejection. However, when letters come winging back week after week, it can take courage and guts to keep going. Deep down, everyone likes to think that their book will be accepted by the first person who reads it.

Writing is a business the same as anything else. What differentiates the winners is the way in which they cope with the adversity and challenges. There's a quote by the late American sports coach Vince Lombardi which sums it all up: "Winners don't quit: quitters don't win".

You have a choice. You can give up and tuck your manuscript under your bed. Or you can see rejection as a necessary part of the process.

Innovation

Here are some suggestions for some of the innovative steps you can take while waiting for an acceptance from an agent:

- Create a blog or e-zine to build up hype about your book.

- Create your own newsletter to keep in touch with your readers.

- Start gathering expert endorsements for your book jacket.

- Provide 'taster' chapters for your forthcoming book on your website.

- Set up your own fan page on social media sites such as Facebook and Twitter.

- Post sample chapters of your book on literary forums – and invite comments from other readers.

- Make a simple recording of yourself reading sample chapters from your book. Put this up on YouTube.

- Start your own virtual book tour. Read sample chapters of your book on webinars and tele-seminars.

- Make a list of people who may be willing to help you promote your book. These may be bloggers or e-zine editors or experts in a similar field.

All these steps are empowering and will prove useful when your book is eventually launched. They will also impress literary agents who will see that you are 100 per cent committed to marketing and promoting your writing.

Many agents and publishers nowadays are asking about an author's social media following before they will commit to a book. Some publishers even specify a minimum of 3,000 followers. Remember the adage about eating an elephant? If you systematically spend 5-10 minutes per day working on this, your numbers will quickly build up.

Inspiring Success Stories

I am including a few of the more awe-inspiring success stories to show you what can be achieved with a tenacity, faith and courage. Largely due to space, I have had to be selective – I could have easily written a separate book devoted solely to these writers. I hope they will inspire you as much as they do me:

- Screen writer Kenya Cagle went to the Cannes Film Festival in an attempt to cold-sell a script written 15 years previously. He had sent 'The Undercover Man' out to more than 100 movie studios. Not one responded. When he came home from Cannes in 2001, he had a $5 million production deal.

- Pennsylvania dentist, entrepreneur, and author, Dr. Joe Capista, reached Number 1 bestseller status on Amazon by using an online viral and marketing campaign. His book, *What Can a Dentist Teach You About Business, Life and Success?* climbed the charts after a virtual blog tour; a video book trailer; internet social networking and forum postings.

- Roddy Doyle's first novel *The Commitments* received much acclaim when it was self-published. It was adapted into a hit movie four years later, catapulting its Irish author into the limelight.

- Charles Frazier self-published his debut novel *Cold Mountain* which was later made into a Hollywood blockbuster starring Nicole Kidman, Jude Law and Renee Zellweger. The book made publishing history when it sailed to the top of *The New York Times* bestseller list for 61 weeks.

- Stephen Clarke decided to self-publish 200 copies of his novel *A Year in Merde* after publishers failed to recognise the potential of his pitch. Within a few months, he'd resold the rights to a major publisher and it eventually sold 175 thousand copies in the UK.

- Professional wildlife photographers Carl Sams and Jean Stoick achieved bestseller status for a book they were told would never sell. Today, there are more than a million copies of *Stranger in the Woods* in print. It's won seven awards and spent 26 weeks on the *New York Times* bestseller list.

- Paul Tawrell believed so much in his book that he sold his house and paid a Canadian printer $125,000 for 35,000 copies. This proved a brilliant move. *Camping & Wilderness Survival* sold over 320,000 copies.

- After rejections from 26 publishers, Vicki Stringer self-published her novel using donations from family and friends. *Let That Be the Reason* sold 1,000 copies from her car boot in the first three weeks. By 2005, her estimated sales leapt to 1.8 million! She now publishes 16 other authors.

- A mere 1000 copies of *Rich Dad, Poor Dad* were printed when it was self-published by co-authors Robert Kiyosaki and Sharon L. Lechter in 1997. The book has since been on most of the bestseller lists and to date has sold 26 million copies around the world.

- Fantasy novel *Eragon* catapulted its teenage author to stardom after it was self-published. After over a year hand-selling his book from town to town, Christopher Paolini, finally received a six-figure deal for the novel and two sequels. His lucky break came after a novelist bought the book and told his publisher about it. The novel has since been made into a film starring Jeremy Irons.

- *You Can Heal Your Life*, privately published by Louise Hay, led to the establishment of Hay House Publishing. This enabled her to publish hundreds of books and audiotapes by other authors who are now household names.

- *The Celestine Prophecy*, a spiritual and self-discovery adventure, was originally self-published by James Redfield. Acquired by Warner books for $800,000, it sold more than 20 million copies worldwide and was translated into 34 languages. The book's initial success was attributed to the author's rigorous lecture schedule.

- *The Christmas Box* made publishing history with of advance of $4 million for a self-published title. Author Richard Paul Evans has since authored many subsequent bestsellers.

- Marketing genius, Joe Karbo, used full page newspaper adverts to attract global sales for his book *The Lazy Man's Way to Riches*. Joe's investment was less than $3,000. He sold nine million dollars worth – though his book was never in a bookstore!

- Vicky Lansky's children's recipe book, *Feed Me, I'm Yours*, was rejected by 49 publishers. It sold 300,000 copies after being self-published. After Bantam took it over, it sold eight million more! Vicky now has more than 30 books to her credit and a very successful small press.

- *The Personal Computer Book,* published by the late author Peter McWilliams, sold over 1.6 million copies. McWilliams also had other bestsellers and sold 3.5 million copies of his self-published poetry books. He was rumored to have refused a one million dollar offer for his publishing company before he died.

The Silver Lining

So much for rejection, rejection, rejection! For these authors, it was the very catalyst that spring-boarded them to success. Without it, they might have had very different lives.

To quote film director, George Lucas: "In my experience, there is no such thing as luck." Anyone who is committed and determined, will make their own luck and good fortune.

What Next?

Here are some suggestions that may be helpful:

- Remember not to take rejection personally. The fact that an agent or editor hasn't accepted your book yet doesn't mean it's rubbish, only that it isn't suitable for their list.

- Remind yourself that rejection is something that's happened to many bestselling and famous writers. Expect obstacles and learn from any setbacks.

- Train yourself to think positively. Focus on growing yourself bigger than your challenges. Remind yourself that you are taking small steps each day towards your goals.

- Each rejection takes you a step closer to finding the right publisher. If someone has taken the time to read your book, this is a tremendous compliment. Take any praise at face value. Agents and publishers won't waste their time reading your manuscript unless they think it has promise. They won't encourage authors unless they mean it. Although it can be hard to hear criticism, their advice may contain a gem that will help you.

- Write affirmations and read them once a day. Switch negative voices and fears into positives. Eg. "No one will ever publish my book" becomes "Someone wants to publish my book – I just have to find them."

- Join a writers' group. Being around other writers helps to spark fresh ideas and build confidence. You can gain experience of public reading, get critiques of your work, and share experiences. You can quickly and easily find online and offline writers groups simply by searching on Google.

- Attend literary festivals and book fairs to make contacts and glean information. You can build up a strong sense of the type of books that publishers are selling and promoting. You will also benefit from attending talks of professional authors writing in the same genre as your own.

- Subscribe to a monthly writing magazine. There are numerous to choose from that will help keep you abreast of writing competitions, literary awards and prizes. Some of the best known of these publications include: **Writers' News, Writers' Magazine, Writer's Forum,** and **Writer's Digest**. Other publications for the publishing industry are **The Bookseller** and **Publishing News**. All of these contain helpful snippets about publishing your work.

- Apply to writing competitions and see if you can get funding for your project. The Book Trust in the UK publishes an up-to-date guide to literary prizes each year. (Details available at www.booktrust.org.uk.) You can also Google for international writers' awards and bursaries that may be suitable.

- Sign up for mentoring with a successful author or book coach. They will have travelled the same path before you and know the shortcuts. A mentor can offer sound editorial judgment on your writing, identify your blind spots and give constructive advice about what to do next.

- Consider setting up a website or blog to promote your book. You can find a web designer to do this for you, or if you are more technically inclined you can buy an 'off-the-peg' website and do it yourself.

- You can locate affordable professionals at sites such as www.elance.com, www.rentacoder.com and www.hiremymom.com.

- Keep a Journal. What have you learned this week? What challenges have you faced? What achieved the best results? What could you have done differently? How will you reward yourself when you achieve your goals?

Chapter 18

Agent Or Publisher?

Going It Alone

We come now, retrospectively, to the thorny question of whether an agent is necessary at all. There is also the alternative of going it alone in approaching publishers.

There are advantages and disadvantages to both choices. Advocates of each option insist that theirs is the only way. So let's look at some of the pros and cons.

There will always be publishers who won't look at manuscripts unless they come direct from a reputable source, such as a literary agent or a literary consultancy. However, there are plenty of commissioning editors out there who will still look at manuscripts sent directly from authors themselves. This is especially true of the smaller publishers that most agents won't even bother approaching.

As with most things in life, your decision will be a personal one based on your own beliefs, personality and available time. I will therefore present arguments in favour of both sides, and let you make up your own mind.

Advantages of Having an Agent

1. An agent will give you sound advice about publishing and publishers. You might not like the advice they give you, but it will be good advice based on the current state of the market.

2. Agents have a notebook full of influential contacts around the world. They know what's in fashion and what's not. If they know of a scout looking for your type of manuscript, this is your shortcut past the slush pile.

3. Literary agents are skilled negotiators. They know how much a book is worth and don't mind haggling over prices – a skill most writers won't possess.

4. There is so much more to selling a book, than simply naming a price. There are serial rights, film rights, foreign rights, digital rights, marketing, etc. included in the average contract. Agents have experience in negotiating all these areas. If you are fortunate enough to be in an auction situation, they are skilled in tickling up prices and managing these too.

5. Marketing and promotion are an important part of any book deal. It's no good having a fantastic book if no one knows about it. A good agent will ensure you get the best marketing deal possible included in your contract.

6. When it comes to selling book rights around the world or negotiating film rights, agents win hands down. There is no way the average writer will ever possess the comprehensive knowledge and influential contacts to ensure their book is published in 65 different languages!

7. An agent leverages your workload. You no longer have to waste hours of your precious writing time on researching publishers. You don't have to do copious amounts of printing and correspondence. Agents cut down on time-consuming paperwork and administration. OK, you pay for the privilege. But if they land you a decent book deal, it's worth every penny. This leaves you more time for your writing – which ultimately is what many authors want.

8. An agent can give you up-to-the-minute advice about a publishing house or editor, based on previous experience. They are not emotionally involved in your book and can see the bigger picture.

9. An agent provides continuity for your career. A good agent will give you a degree of guidance and nurturing. If you represent yourself and switch from publisher to publisher, you simply won't get this.

10. An agent can act as an intermediary or a buffer with your publisher. Instead of irritating or annoying a particular editor with your requests (you may not like your front cover, for example, or you may disagree with an editor's amendments) then an agent can smooth over any potential areas of disagreement.

11. Many writers are just so grateful to be getting published that they blow negotiations. They may be too eager to say, "yes please" to a mediocre offer. Or alternatively, they may be mortally offended by an offer they don't like. Body language and mannerisms can be a giveaway for the inexperienced.

Lack of experience or over-negotiation can lead to you losing deals with publishers. Alternatively, you may mistakenly accept deals that are unfair. The case springs to mind of a client who came to me for help a while back. He'd just sold his non-fiction book on Muhammad Ali to a publisher for £500. The book contained true stories about the boxer's home life and exclusive photographs never seen before. Given Ali's worldwide following and fan base of millions, the potential readership was huge. The writer was in despair, wishing he'd never signed away his book rights for such a paltry sum. Working together, we came up with a plan that enabled him to legally get out of his contract. Fortunately, he was able to walk away from the deal, and it is now a 'boxing' bestseller. However, things could so easily have turned out rather differently.

12. Book contracts can be complex. They can contain clauses detailing hardback royalties; paperback royalties; cheap editions, premium sales and remainders, book club and condensed book rights, electronic and audio editions, and subsidiary rights.

A typical clause might state: *The publisher shall pay the Author the following royalties: of the British published price on all copies sold, excluding such copies as may be specified in subsequent clauses of this agreement: 10% on the first 2500 copies sold; 12.5% on the next 2,500; and 15% on all copies sold thereafter.*

The average writer is unlikely to know if 10% or 20% is standard and fair.

Disadvantages of Agents

1. Agents take around 10 per cent commission for home sales; 20 per cent for international sales. If you represent yourself, you won't have to share the loot with anyone else.

2. Agents tend to have an emphasis, spoken or unspoken, on sales. As a result, agents can be resistant to less commercial fields of writing. If they're going to spend day and night flogging a book, they want to know they've earned enough to cover their time and expenses. If you see yourself as an *artiste* rather than a mass-market author, you may prefer to represent yourself in order to focus on less commercial writing.

3. Many agents won't bother approaching smaller independent publishers who pay lower advances for books. Anyone paying less than £5,000 for a book really isn't going to be worth their while. So if you have written a book for a small niche market – for example, an academic text or a book aimed at a narrow specialist field - then it may work in your favour to represent yourself.

4. Different agents have different policies to rejection. Some will approach a dozen publishers before calling it a day, and asking the writer to start another book. Others will keep going. While this can be frustrating for the writer, remember that this ultimately boils down to a balancing act between payment and work. Agents aren't charities. They can't keep sending out a book if there appears to be no prospect of getting paid – and largely, a lot of their efforts do go unpaid.

Obviously, if you're representing yourself you can keep going for as long as it takes. You have complete control over the entire process and won't feel at the mercy of someone else's decision-making.

5. Last but not least, finding an agent is no walk in the park! It can be just as hard to get your book taken on by a literary agent, as it is to get it accepted by a publisher. Once you have signed a contract with a literary agency, there may be another long wait while publishers are approached.

Chapter 19

The Magic Of A One-Line Pitch

Why It's Essential

Imagine you've just stepped into an elevator with a famous film director. He has several billion dollars in his bank account and is looking for the next hot script. You have around 60 seconds to sell your book. What will you say? Will you be prepared or speechless?

More realistically, imagine you are introduced to an international talent scout at a book launch. S/he is about to leave, but you have time before the taxi arrives to arouse his/her interest. If you had to summarise your book in one sentence only, what would it be?

You might be thinking: 'This is absurd. Neither of those things is likely to happen to me. Besides, I need more than one sentence to sum up my book.'

Not so! It is a widely held belief in the industry that bestsellers can be sold on one sentence alone. If you doubt this, think of the clever one-line sales pitches that may have prompted you to buy books or see movies in the past. Often, three words evoke a theme or mood. Sometimes, it is just *one* word.

Examples of one-line sales pitches for bestselling books

- A schoolboy spends the first ten years of his life sleeping under the stairs of a family that hates him - then discovers he's a wizard!

Harry Potter and the Philosopher's Stone – J.K. Rowling

- Sleep-deprived parents can learn how to get their baby to sleep through the night by the time they're ten weeks old.

  The New Contented Little Baby Book – Gina Ford

- How to cheat at cooking amazing meals if you haven't got the time or experience.

  How to Cheat at Cooking – Delia Smith

- A killer and genius has an extraordinary gift: a sense of smell more powerful than any other human's.

  Perfume – Patrick Suskind

Practice Your Pitch

The purpose of the following exercises is to focus your mind and fine-tune your abilities so that you're thinking like a pro.

You will soon have a one-line pitch perfected so that every time you're asked about your book, you'll be able to confidently promote yourself and your work. Once you have a pitch, use it and rehearse it. You can practice on family members, colleagues at work, and acquaintances at social functions.

There are numerous uses for your pitch. You may be trying to coax the manager of a local bookstore to stock your book or hold a reading. You may be cajoling a book reviewer from your local newspaper to read your novel. You might be phoning a producer at a local radio station to try to drum up publicity. You may be taking part in a panel discussion at a prestigious literary festival. One day, you might even be interviewed on a prime-time TV show!

The goal is to get your pitch down to one sentence. If any words or information are unnecessary, get rid of them. The golden rule is: if in doubt, strip it out.

What Next?

Exercise One

Write one-line sales pitches for ten of your favourite books. These can include both non-fiction and fiction.

This should get you thinking about what should and shouldn't be included in a pitch.

Exercise Two

Write three different one-line sales pitches for your own book. (Choose a different angle for each if possible).

Exercise Three

i) Rehearse your pitch in front of the mirror or using a dictaphone. This may feel slightly awkward at first. However, persevere until you feel more comfortable with the exercise.

ii) You can warm up your voice very simply by making the following sounds as you exhale. Hold on to the note until you run out of breath. This should clear any 'croaks' out of your voice:

oooooooooooooooh...

eeeeeeeeeeeeeeee...

yuuuuuuuuuuuuuu...

mmmmmmmmmm...

And no, I've not gone bonkers. These are the vocal sounds used by many professional broadcasters, actors, and speakers to warm up before they perform!

iii) Practice saying the words with a smile, as this transfers to your voice. This helps your listener to relax as they feel in safe hands.

Smiles confer confidence and self-assurance. You have every reason to feel assured. You've accomplished something remarkable that many other people only dream about. You should feel proud of yourself. This is your moment to shine. Enjoy it.

Chapter 20

Your First Meeting

Preparation Is Everything

So you have the interest of a literary agent or publisher. Brilliant news! You will rightly be thrilled to bits. In all the buzz and excitement, prepare for your first meeting with the same meticulous detail as you would for a job interview.

It's rare for an author to meet their publisher face-to-face. Pressure of time means that the closest you're likely to get is a couple of brisk phone conversations or a series of emails.

Alternatively, your agent may handle this side of proceedings. The majority of my advice is therefore going to be geared towards a meeting with a literary agent. However, parts of it will be applicable to a publisher too.

What They Are Looking For?

First of all, let's consider a literary agent's aims in arranging a meeting with you. Their number one priority will be to find out more about you and to size up your short- and long-term prospects. They'll want to know how 'marketable' you are as an author (you're part of the marketing too remember).

They'll be asking themselves whether you have experience of public speaking; whether you're easy to get along with; whether you're likely to dry up in front of a microphone or an audience.

They'll want to know what your long-term plans are, such as

ideas for your next book or books. In this way, they can establish whether their best course of action is to sell (in the case of an agent) or buy (in the case of a publisher) your current book or to attempt a two-book deal or even a three-book deal.

They'll also be keen to know about your writing routine – whether it takes you 12 months to write a book or five years. It will be useful to let them know of any other commitments you may have. This will be important if there are deadlines to meet.

They'll also take note of how receptive you are to criticism, and how responsive you seem to suggestions that they make. They'll also be interested to know how you perceive your own book and if you have any ideas for marketing it.

Have Answers Ready

It's essential to have answers prepared so that you're not caught off-guard. No slipping into a bar beforehand for a quick drink to bolster your nerves. No mind-altering substances either, please. There is little more off-putting than sitting opposite someone with glazed eyes or who is a little tipsy.

Bear in mind that if you seem too rigid or inflexible, this may not work in your favour. Similarly, you should not be too defensive about any criticisms of your book, even if you disagree. Your instant response may be that you do not wish to write or publish anything that feels fundamentally against your principles.

In such instances, it's best to go away and reflect first before giving a final answer. For example, one of my mentees was asked to rewrite her radio script with the heroine as a hero. Her first response was outrage, but after weighing up the deal involved, she eventually relented and agreed to do this. While she disliked making the changes, she got an opportunity that she would not otherwise have had. The choice was simple: a rewrite in return for a reputable contract, or sticking to her guns and getting no deal at all.

Know Your Boundaries

Everyone is different. A screenwriter I know was so offended by the sexist rewrite suggested by a director that she turned the offer down outright. The script has never appeared on television as a result – but she is happy with that. What she could not have lived with was the prospect of her manuscript being changed beyond recognition and having her name attached to it. No amount of money or fame would have persuaded her otherwise.

A Two-Book Deal

Though a two-book deal may sound like a distant dream, it's worth giving this some serious thought beforehand. Think seriously about whether a deadline would motivate you or if such pressure would be more likely to make you freeze up.

Consider other commitments or circumstances in your personal life that might impact on your ability to deliver to a deadline. A client of mine was contracted to complete her second novel immediately after her first child was conceived. She had an unexpectedly difficult pregnancy – but she had committed to write the book. She felt the quality suffered as a result, and regretted signing the contact.

How would you cope if life threw something at you unexpectedly? Are you over-stretched already? Or do you have sufficient time and support to glide over any rough patches?

Checklist

Here is a quick checklist of questions you may wish to ask a literary agent:

- What do you like about my book?
- What do you suggest as areas in need of improvement?
- Do you have anyone specific in mind who may be interested?
- How many publishers will you send it to before giving up?
- Who will you be sending it to first?
- Will you send the manuscript out one at a time, or six at a time?
- How would you envisage my manuscript being marketed?
- Timescale – what sort of time frame will be involved in selling my book? Is it likely to take twelve weeks or twelve months?
- How confident are you of selling my book?
- Point of contact – who is my point of contact? Is it you or do you have an assistant?
- Updates – how regularly will I be updated on progress?

- Will I receive copies of rejection letters or hear about publishers' feedback? (Different agents have different policies for this).

- Do you have other plans for my book? Will you be passing it on to your foreign rights and film rights departments?

- Contract – can I see a sample copy of your contract before signing it?

- Are you interested in plans for my next book? (Take along a synopsis or pitch if you have one.)

An Amicable Relationship

Writing is a lonely profession and it can be easy to strike up friendships with anyone who shows an interest in your work. However, it's in your best interests to keep the relationship with your agent on business-like terms.

This may sound obvious. However, over the years, I've heard too many agents and publishers complain of clients using them as counsellors or emotional punch bags. They don't want calls in the middle of the day to discuss writer's block or your relationship problems. They don't necessarily want intense discussions about your plans for your next three books. Mainly they want a professional, successful, amicable, and hopefully enduring business relationship. This will largely be based on your skill in writing books and their ability to sell them.

The key thing to remember is that your agent is not your counsellor, your confidante nor even your friend. Never forget this fact when you are sitting in their office or hanging on the other end of the phone. Treat them with as much respect as a bank manager or a business colleague, and you will have a happy partnership for many years to come.

Remember also that agents and publishers, like the rest of us, are not immune to flattery. If you can talk to them engagingly, showing that you know a little about them and their work, this will go down well. It also helps if you can emphasise that you particularly want to be represented or published by them.

What Next?

Exercise One

Research the literary agent or publisher. Find out who they represent and what sort of books they have had published in the past.

Exercise Two

Prepare a list of questions to take along with you.

Chapter 21

When To Hassle, When To Hold Fire

Troubleshooting

You've got your literary agent and you're on top of the world. But as time passes, things just seem to be happening too slowly.

Why haven't you heard anything? Have they sent your manuscript out? Are they messing you around? Do they treat all their clients this way?

Annoyance and irritation starts to bubble up. That feeling of gratitude you felt when you signed their contract, starts to fade away.

When will they DO something? When will you get your book deal?

What To Do

As agents make their living from the percentage earned by selling your book, they'll do their utmost to find a publisher for it.

In the meantime, they're spending their own money to do this - which should be treated as a tremendous privilege rather than an automatic 'right'. Nagging or grumbling is unlikely to speed things along.

If you work in a lightning-quick industry or a profession priding itself on speed of service, you may find the waiting unbearable. However, if you continually harass an agent, it's likely to result in a letter saying something like: *"We haven't yet succeeded in placing your book. After due consideration, we feel that perhaps you should seek representation elsewhere."*

If you have heard nothing from them within six to eight weeks (which often seems quite standard) make a brief phone call or write an amicable follow-up email.

Remember that there is a fine line between persistence and pestering. Do not keep sending your agent revised copies of your "improved" manuscript. Do not keep phoning to "discuss" your book. Do not keep emailing them with your ideas and questions.

Any signs of hectoring, nagging or obsessiveness may make them think twice about your prospects as a client. They'll also find a home for your manuscript much quicker if they're left to get on with their job.

Make The Most Of This Time

Use this time as an opportunity to do some reading, to set new goals for yourself, or to dream up new marketing ideas. You might even start planning out your next book!

Conclusion

Live Your Dreams

Visualise Your Success

Close your eyes: imagine holding your book in your hands for the first time. Feel how smooth and shiny the cover is. Flick the pages and feel the breeze from the paper tickle your cheeks. Now turn back the cover and see your name on the opening page.

Who will you share this precious moment with? How will you celebrate? Will you crack open the bubbly? Will you phone your parents and children? Or will you whoop and holler so loud you're heard several streets away?

A few weeks before writing this guide, a writer came to see me at The Oxford Literary Consultancy. She'd received rejection after rejection for her first novel. Not one agent – not a single one - had been interested in reading her manuscript. "I know I'm doing something wrong. I just need to know what it is," she said.

As I chatted to this writer, I could see that she had a burning desire to see her work in print and that she was prepared to do whatever it took to achieve it. Like so many writers, she'd stayed at her computer while her friends went out to the pub. She'd snatched time to write during her lunch breaks. She'd given up weekends and holidays.

We spent the day discussing what she needed to do to get her work noticed. Then, together, we rewrote her synopsis, covering letter and author biography.

This morning, I received a postcard from her. It simply said: *Nine agents have asked for my manuscript. Those are just the ones I've heard back from.*

Her story is little different to that of the many writers I speak to every day. There was nothing remarkable about it, but the fortuitous timing.

But guess what? The secrets I shared with her are the same ones I'm sharing with you.

The exact same thing can happen to you…

Sources

Many thanks for materials taken from:

Northern Lights (copyright, Philip Pullman, 1995) the first part of his **Dark Materials** trilogy, published by Scholastic Children's Books. Reproduced by kind permission of Scholastic Ltd. All rights reserved.

I Can Make You Rich by Paul McKenna, published by Bantam Press. Reprinted by kind permission of The Random House Group.

Feast by Nigella Lawson, published by Chatto & Windus. Reprinted by kind permission of The Random House Group.

With special thanks to my clients:

Louise Soraya Black, award-winning author of **Pomegranate Sky** *(Aurora Metro, 2010)*

Sarah Loving, author of **Too Gross, Too True** *(Picadilly Press, 2010)*

Tom Broadbent, author of **On Younghusband's Path** *(Headhunter, 2005)*

The Author

Stephanie J. Hale is a writing coach and publishing expert who has worked with fiction and non-fiction authors for over 20 years – helping them to write, sell and promote their books.

She is author of award-winning books including: *Millionaire Author, How to Sell One Million Books* and *Millionaire Property Author.*

She is former Assistant Director of the world-famous creative writing course at Oxford University. She founded Oxford Literary Consultancy in 2004.

She was awarded a British Empire Medal for services to authors by Her Majesty the Queen in 2017.

The Authors' Vault
FREE Training and Bonuses
Specially for You

- Topics include:
- How to Find a Publisher or Literary Agent.
- How to Choose a Bestselling Book Title.
- Mistakes to Avoid with Agents and Publishers.
- Red Flags to Look Out For in a Publishing Contract.
- How to Write a Marketing Plan for Your Book.
- Can I Quote Someone Without Permission?
- Should I Use 50 Shades of X as a Book Title?
- How to Write Your Book Faster.
- How to Choose the Best Book Cover.
- Should I Self-Publish or is a Mainstream Publisher Better?
- How to Sell More Copies of your Book.
- How to Stop Other Authors Stealing Your Book Idea.
- Should I Disguise Real-Life Characters?
- How to Get Celebrity Endorsements.
- And much more ...

Register for your free reports at:

www.CelebrityAuthorsSecrets.com/vault

Oxford Literary Consultancy
Publishing Services

- Manuscript evaluation – confidential feedback of your book's marketability.

- Proofreading and editing – with fast-track service.

- Book cover design and typesetting.

- PR campaigns – publicity in magazines, newspapers, radio and TV.

- Ghostwriting.

- Mentoring.

Our consultants work for publishers including: Bloomsbury, HarperCollins, Hodder & Stoughton, Little Brown, Simon & Schuster and Random House.

Find out whether your book idea is marketable.

Book a free 20-minute consultation today!

www.oxfordwriters.com